CUCINA CLASSICA

Maintaining a Tradition

D1611698

Order Sons of Italy in America
New York Grand Lodge Foundation, Inc.
Bellmore, New York 11710-5605

The proceeds of this book will be used by the Order Sons of Italy in America, New York Grand Lodge Foundation, Inc. for the purposes of funding the cultural, educational and philanthropic programs of the Grand Lodge of the State of New York. Many thanks for your support of the Order Sons of Italy in America, the oldest and largest organization of Italian-American Men and Women in the United States and Canada.

ISBN 0-9647376-0-4

First Printing   February 1995
Second Printing   June 1995
Third Printing   October 1997
Fourth Printing   January 2001
Fifth Printing September 2001
Sixth Printing   August 2002
Seventh Printing   January 2003
Eighth Printing September 2003

Additional copies may be obtained at the cost of $16.95 per book, plus $3.75 postage and handling. Send to:

Order Sons of Italy in America
New York Grand Lodge Foundation, Inc.
2101 Bellmore Avenue
Bellmore, New York 11710-5605

WIMMER
COOKBOOKS

ConsolidatedGraphics
1-800-548-2537

TABLE OF CONTENTS

HISTORY

Order Sons of Italy in America

In the nineteenth century, America saw the rapid growth of mutual aid societies throughout all sectors of society, including both the native born and immigrants. For immigrants, the mutual aid society provided a familiar setting where their dialect was spoken and old world customs recreated.

So, the idea of uniting Italians in one great organization, which would enable them to become authorities of their own destinies and progress, came to Dr. Vincenzo Sellaro around 1904. With the help of five trusted friends, a pharmacist Ludovico Ferrari, a lawyer Antonio Marzullo, a sculptor Giuseppe Carlino, and two barbers Pietro Viscardi and Robert Merlo, he proceeded to organize the Italian immigrant population.

It was on June 22, 1905 that the first act of incorporation took place and the organization became known as the "Supreme Lodge of the Sons of Italy". It was their desire to attract and exert a great impact on fellow Italian immigrants, most of whom were single and uncultured folks, in that Dr. Sellaro introduced a fraternal organization with a ritual ceremony, altar and officers. The Order from the very day of its birth was, and always has been, loyal to its non-political and non-denominational beliefs.

The years that followed furnished evidence attesting to and confirming the vitality of the Order, beginning with the increasing number of lodges formed. Because the Order had enlarged its program, its activities multiplied and membership grew. The Order acquired custody over the relic most dear to the hearts of Italians in America: the Garibaldi Pantheon in Staten Island. For years it had been neglected and abandoned to such a point that urgent repairs were required to save it from complete destruction. After long negotiations it was finally ceded to the Sons of Italy. No organization in America, other than the Order, could have expressed the sense of veneration and affection that immigrants felt for the house that once sheltered the "Hero of the Two Worlds."

In the years that followed the number of grand or state lodges increased, many programs were established, i.e., low cost insurance programs, death benefits, funds for widows, invalids, and orphans, and citizenship classes were conducted. Some of these same programs are still in existence today.

In 1931, a large delegation of OSIA leaders met with President Hoover on the White House lawn. In succeeding administrations the OSIA has had the pleasure of meeting with Presidents Truman, Nixon, Carter, Reagan and Bush. President Carter addressed the Order's 1979 National Convention in Baltimore, Maryland. In 1942 the position of OSIA National Deputy was created to lobby for the Order in Washington, D.C.

In the early 1940's scholarships for college students were established and for the past five decades there has been a greater support for education.

The National OSIA Foundation was created in 1959 as a conduit for funding charitable projects and supporting other projects of the Order.

From 1904 to 1955 the Supreme Headquarters had been in New York, later moved to Philadelphia and in 1981 relocated to Washington, D.C. In 1982, OSIA purchased a building in Washington that serves as the National Office with an Executive Director and staff.

Early in its history ... in 1920 ... OSIA offered women complete parity and many of its local lodges have had either all female or co-ed membership. In 1931 the first woman was elected Supreme Trustee. Fifty years later, women began to occupy top officer positions and at the August 1993 National Convention, Joanne L. Strollo was elected as the first woman National President.

Over all these passing years, the Order has continued to both encourage the maintenance of Italian culture and language, as well as encourage assimilation into American social and political life. The Order Sons of Italy in America has sponsored a wide variety of programs over these many years ... banks, savings and loan, credit unions, social halls/lodge buildings, senior citizen housing, newspapers, citizenship classes, political action groups, Commission for Social Justice, Columbus Day and Italian Heritage events. The history of the Order not only contributes to our Italian American experience but helps clarify the larger issues of ethnic, community and politics in America, as well as preserving our proud heritage.

Today, with approximately 90,000 members and a sizable social and fraternal membership in 800 local lodges, the Order Sons of Italy in America remains the largest and most geographically representative organization of Italians and Italian Americans in the United States and Canada.

Please see the final pages for information on how to become a member of OSIA.

Spring 1995

Happy 90th!

For some 90 years, L'Ordine Figli d'Italia in America, or as we today call ourselves, the Order Sons, and Daughters, of Italy in America, has weathered and withstood the span of time. We are a unique grassroots and community based organization of Italian American men and women, grounded in the firm belief that Liberty, Equality and Fraternity are our most precious prerogatives.

This commemorative 90th Anniversary Cookbook is the culmination of many hours of dedicated work by volunteers who shared a vision in that our rich culinary past as Italians and Italian-Americans could be combined with our rich history and lodges and members of the OSIA. Indeed, this publication is a tribute to our beloved founder, Dr. Vincenzo Sellaro, who on June 22, 1905 began a legacy in Little Italy, New York City, by attempting to unite all Italians and Italian Americans under one umbrella organization in these United States. We keep his dream alive today in our many lodges.

May you enjoy your hours of culinary reading pleasure and your hours of cooking. Think often of us all as Figli d'Italia — the Children of Italy, who today recommit ourselves in *"Keeping a Promise: Maintaining a Tradition."*

Our gratitude to all who contributed their favorite recipes, to the lodges for their living witness to the history of our New York State OSIA and special thanks to Rose Albertson and Nancy Quinn for their execution of this terrific publication. You make us ever so proud of our culture and heritage.

Buon appetito and sempre avanti!

Joseph Sciame
State President
Grand Lodge of New York

90TH ANNIVERSARY COMMEMORATIVE COOKBOOK COMMITTEE

Co-Chairpersons
Rose Albertson   Nancy Quinn

Honorary State Committee
Matilda Cuomo   Susan Molinari

State OSIA Committee
Lucy F. Codella
Rosemarie Montemarano
Chris Parillo
Sophie Sciame
Edith Zuzolo

District OSIA Committee

Joyce Abbate	Valerie Gobbo
Dolores Altomare	Maria Little
Mary Ann Barone	Susan Mele
Gloria Ciancaglini	Theresa Neville
Marcy Dabbene	Jennie Tompkins
Laura De Sario	Nardina Trotta
Mary Daniels	Catherine Ward
Gloria Enea	Frances Suraci White

New York State Grand Lodge Office Staff
Julianne Sirianni
Rosalie Galatioto
Joanne Gomez

Resource Advisor
Maria D'Urso

Divider Art
Denise Gangi

Cover Art Illustration and Design
Cheryl Prochilo

90th Anniversary New York State OSIA Chairperson
Peter R. Zuzolo

New York State OSIA President
Joseph Sciame

ACKNOWLEDGMENTS AND GRAZIE

When we celebrate anniversaries, we look forward to receiving that special personalized greeting card followed by a special celebration meal. This publication is our "Anniversary Greeting" to the Order Sons of Italy in America during its 90th Anniversary year ... and within its pages are the ingredients for that special anniversary meal!

Some new and innovative recipes were received from the "youth" of our Order and many have been passed down from generation to generation and have become an integral part of the preservation of our beautiful Italian heritage. We hope you will try some of our recipes ... and always keep a special place in your heart for the familiar foods we all continue to prepare year after year.

Due to space limitations and duplication, we were not able to publish all of the recipes received but we hope to have made the best possible selection to cross-section recipes submitted from all over our great Empire State. Our sincere appreciation to the entire 90th Anniversary Cookbook Committee for their dedication to this project ... and to all our Brothers and Sisters who submitted over 700 recipes for consideration.

Interspersed within the pages of this cookbook is a listing of all the current New York State OSIA lodges along with a short biography on their names. There are many interesting facts about famous Italians and Italian Americans to be "digested" within this cookbook and it is our hope that if you are not already a member of the Order, you will contact one of the lodges in your area and join our ranks!!

Finally, many thanks to our State President Joseph Sciame for the confidence and vision he has given to all of us. It is truly a pleasure to see one of your dreams finalized.

Happy 90th Anniversary to the Order Sons of Italy in America!

Rose Albertson and Nancy Quinn

To Those Who Have Served The Grand Lodge State of New York
Order Sons of Italy in America

- We Salute You On Our 90th Anniversary -

The Founders

Dr. Vincenzo Sellaro
Pietro Viscardi
Ludovico Ferrari
Antonio Marzullo
Roberto Merlo
Giuseppe Carlino

New York City — June 22, 1905

New York State Grand Venerables and State Presidents

Anthony Gulotta 1911	Andrew J. Malatesta 1941 - 1943	P. Vincent Landi 1969 - 1973
Crescenzo Pitocchi 1911 - 1913	Francis X. Giaccone 1943 - 1951	Joseph G. Bologna 1973 - 1975
Stefano Miele 1913 -1917	Ubaldo N. Marino 1951 - 1955	Joseph E. Fay 1975 - 1977
Corrado Stornello 1917 -1921	Amedeo H. Volpe 1955 - 1957	Peter R. Zuzolo 1977 - 1981
Salvatore Cotillo 1921 - 1925	Carmine A. Ventiera 1957 - 1961	Joseph Montemarano 1981 - 1985
John J. Freschi 1925 - 1933	Peter A. Brevett 1961 - 1965	Nicholas G. Viglietta 1985 - 1989
Stefano Miele 1933 - 1935	Salvatore Migliaccio 1965 - 1967	Joseph Parillo, Jr. 1989 - 1993
Frank Catinella 1935 - 1941	George Montopoli 1967 - 1969	Joseph Sciame 1993 - 1995

New York Grand Lodge Foundation, Inc.
Order Sons of Italy in America

The OSIA New York Grand Lodge Foundation, Inc. was created to carry out the cultural, educational and philanthropic endeavors of the Order Sons of Italy in America. Major Foundation programs include:

The Commission for Social Justice, formed to fight bias and stereotyping, particularly in the media and in the depiction of Italian Americans in academic textbooks. It strives to promote positive images of Americans of Italian ancestry through its work in education, business and legal affairs, media and intergroup relations.

The Garibaldi Meucci Museum, a city, state and national landmark, was the home of the Italian inventor Antonio Meucci, from 1850 to 1889. It was also a refuge for the Italian hero of the Wars of the Risorgimento, Giuseppe Garibaldi, from 1850 to 1854. This unique Museum is maintained by the Foundation and has become the focus for the celebration of the rich history of the Italian-American community and its many contributions to the great country which provided refuge and opportunity to so many. The Garibaldi Meucci Museum is located at 420 Tompkins Avenue, Staten Island, New York, and is open to the public Tuesday through Sunday.

Scholarships and Charities — The Foundation conducts an extensive college scholarship program throughout New York State. Also granted each year are funds to numerous charities, such as Cooley's Anemia Foundation, Alzheimer's Foundation, Arthritis Foundation, Boys' and Girls' Towns of Italy, Bone Marrow Registry, Gift of Life program at St. Francis Hospital on Long Island, OSIA Gift of Sight and for many Disaster Relief needs.

BLESSING AND RECIPE

Father Donald B. Licata
State and National Chaplain
Order Sons of Italy in America

"Family, Food, Faith" go hand in hand for the Italian. "Panis Angelicus" (Heavenly Bread) — "Pane Di Vita Eterna" — Bread is always at the heart and the head of a table in an Italian household. When people break bread together, they are at peace. May the "Bread of Life" — May the family unity envisioned around the table be the sign for all to see. May that unity bring peace to a troubled world!

Father Licata's "Misto Di Cielo"
(Heavenly Mixture)

COLOR ... APPEARANCE ... PRESENTATION ... PICTURE IT ALL!!

Genoa Salami thinly sliced in a circle on outer rim of tray.

Ripe tomatoes sliced and placed in second circle.

Fresh mozzarella sliced and placed in third circle.

Red roasted pepper placed in the fourth circle.

Place a cut glass dish filled with **caponata**
(eggplant salad) in center of circle.

Intersperse among the circle, **black Sicilian olives**.

Splash a dash of **balsamic vinegar** over entire tray.

Place side trays of sliced **Sicilian bread** (seeded) adding to the color.

What makes the mixture "heavenly" is the blending of the
different tastes.

Mangia Bene!!

ANTIPASTI

APPETIZERS

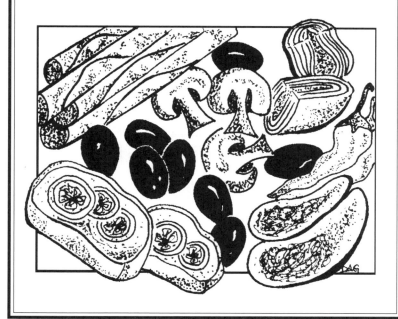

NEW YORK OSIA FILIAL LODGES

•**Uguaglianza Ladies Lodge #83A**, The Bronx, Charter issued 1911: This lodge was named after a portion of our motto, "Equality".

•**Mario Biaggi Lodge #134**, Ozone Park, Charter issued 1976: New York City Police Officer Mario Biaggi was injured eleven times in the line of duty and is the most decorated police officer in the nation with 27 citations. He served 20 years as a Congressman from The Bronx.

•**Grace Fusco Lodge #134A**, Ozone Park, Charter issued 1978: Named after the late wife of National Arbitration Commissioner Rocco C. Fusco, Grace was a devoted wife and mother who passed away while attending a lodge dinner-dance.

•**Giuseppe Mazzini Lodge #137**, Staten Island, Charter issued 1912: Giuseppe Mazzini was a philosopher and evangelical activist mainly responsible for Italy's liberation.

•**Williamsburg Lodge #144**, Brooklyn, Charter issued 1913: This lodge was named after the Williamsburg section of Brooklyn.

•**Guglielmo Marconi Lodge #154**, Corning, Charter issued 1913: In 1897, Guglielmo Marconi, the "Father of Radio" received a patent for "The Wireless" and went on to win the Nobel Prize for Physics in 1909.

•**Verrazano Lodge #212**, Brooklyn, Charter issued 1914: This lodge was named after the famous Italian explorer Giovanni da Verrazzano. The Verrazano Bridge is a land link between Brooklyn and Staten Island, two boroughs of New York City.

•**Antonio Meucci Lodge #213**, White Plains, Charter issued 1914: In 1871, Antonio Meucci from Florence, Italy invented the "Telettrofono", five years before Alexander Graham Bell's patent. In 1980, after 66 years of struggle to raise necessary funds, this lodge completed the construction of a lodge building well known within the White Plains area.

•**Roma Intangible Lodge #215**, Delmar, Charter issued 1913: This lodge was named after the motto of Roman times meaning "Rome was untouchable".

•**Giosue Carducci Lodge #226A**, Hornell, Charter issued 1914: This women's lodge is named after the Italian poet, Giosue Carducci, who was a professor at Bologna University. His works include the rebellious "Inno a Satana" (Hymn to Satan).

•**Alessandro Manzoni Lodge #258**, Mamaroneck, Charter issued 1914: Alessandro Manzoni was an Italian author (1785-1873) famous for his romantic novel "I Promesi Sposi". He wrote many plays and notable religious poetry. Napoleon's death inspired his "Cinque Maggio".

•**Gabriele D'Annunzio Lodge #321**, Schenectady, Charter issued 1915: Gabriele D'Annunzio was a famous Italian soldier, novelist and poet.

•**Dante Alighieri Lodge #436**, Oswego, Charter issued 1915: Dante Alighieri (1265-1321) was an Italian poet born in Florence, Italy and known as the "Father of the Italian Language". His most famous work is "Divine Comedy".

•**Duca Degli Abbruzzi Lodge #443**, Endicott, Charter issued 1915: This lodge was named after a famous Duke of Abruzzi, Luigi Amadeo who was an Italian naval officer, mountain climber and explorer.

(Continued on next divider page)

MOZZARELLA IN CARROZZA

¼-inch thick slices of mozzarella   **sliced bread, egg, and butter**

Cut ¼-inch thick slices of mozzarella, place these mozzarella slices between two slices of bread, press together forming a sandwich. In lightly beaten egg, dip the sandwich, on both sides. In lightly buttered pan, fry gently, first on one side then on the other side until the mozzarella is melted.

Serve hot.

Mary Spinelli Crescetelli
William C. La Morte Lodge #2251

PEPPERONI QUICHE

Prebake pie shell for 10 minutes. Be sure to prick holes first.

¾ cup shredded Swiss cheese   **1 cup thinly sliced pepperoni**
¾ cup mozzarella cheese, cut up or shredded

Spread on precooked pie shell, then mix the next four ingredients.

3 small eggs or 2 large ones   **¼ teaspoon oregano**
1 cup half and half cream   **1 teaspoon chopped parsley**

Mix 4 above ingredients and pour over cheese and mozzarella mix and bake in 350° oven for 35 to 45 minutes.

Pauline Nocella
Italo Balbo Lodge #2361

COCKTAIL MEATBALLS ITALIANO

1 pound ground beef
¾ cup Italian style bread
   crumbs
½ cup chopped onions
¼ cup grated Parmesan cheese
½ cup water
1 egg, lightly beaten

1 clove garlic, minced
½ teaspoon salt
⅛ teaspoon black pepper
¼ cup Italian olive oil
1 (15 ounce) can tomato sauce
⅓ cup packed brown sugar
½ cup red wine vinegar

In large bowl combine ground beef, ¼ cup bread crumbs, onion, cheese, water, egg, garlic, salt and pepper. Shape meatballs with one level tablespoon meat mixture. Coat meatballs with remaining bread crumbs. In large skillet, heat olive oil, add meatballs, cook 5 to 7 minutes, turning occasionally to brown all sides, drain. In small bowl, combine tomato sauce, brown sugar and vinegar, pour over meatballs. Cover, simmer 20 minutes, stirring occasionally.

Olga V. Pacil
Geneva American Italian Ladies Lodge #2397A

MARINATED RAW MUSHROOMS

1 pound raw mushrooms,
   cleaned and finely sliced
juice of 1 lemon
2 tablespoons olive oil
1 teaspoon sugar
2 tablespoons finely chopped
   parsley

salt and pepper to taste
½ cup vegetable oil
1 tablespoon white wine
   vinegar
½ cup finely chopped scallions
1 tablespoon prepared mustard

Moisten the mushrooms with the lemon juice the minute you slice them to prevent darkening. Put the oils, mustard, vinegar and sugar in a blender and blend well. Pour over the sliced mushrooms, add the scallions and parsley. Season with salt and pepper and toss well. Chill and serve on bed of lettuce.
Serves approximately 4.

Frances DeSilva
Italo Balbo Lodge #2361

BAKED CLAMS

½ cup margarine
2 cloves garlic, minced
4 stalks celery, chopped
1 can cream of mushroom soup
3 cans minced clams, drained
1 tablespoon parsley
½ teaspoon oregano

1 tablespoon Worcestershire
  sauce
5 shakes Tabasco sauce
seasoned bread crumbs
paprika
Parmesan cheese

Sauté garlic and celery in margarine until soft. Add remaining ingredients, stir in undiluted soup last. Simmer 5 minutes. Add seasoned bread crumbs until thick. Spoon into clam shells (aluminum shells can be purchased at party supply stores). Sprinkle with cheese and then paprika. Bake at 375° for 30 minutes until bubbles.
Makes 36 clams.

Can be made ahead of time and/or frozen, then baked.

Myra Pappania
Aida Ladies Lodge #2163A

OLIVE BRUSCHETTA

1 loaf Italian bread
1 (5¼ ounce) jar olive paste, or
  canned olives, drained and
  chopped finely

roasted red peppers, drained
  and chopped finely

Cut eight ½-inch thick slices from 1 loaf of Italian bread. Spread each with 1 to 2 teaspoons olive paste or drained and chopped canned olives. Drain and finely chop enough roasted red peppers to make about 2 tablespoons (jar or homemade); divide among bruschetta.

Sybil DeSimone
Romanesque Lodge #2198

RAE'S BRUSCHETTA

1 loaf regular French bread, cut in half lengthwise

6 ounces Portobello mushrooms (chop ¾ cup of mushrooms leaving large pieces aside)

¾ cup chopped onions

3 cloves garlic, chopped

1 medium firm tomato, chopped

½ cup locatelli or any similar grated cheese

2-3 tablespoons fresh parsley, chopped

2-3 tablespoons fresh basil, chopped

½ cup olive oil

After slicing bread lengthwise, place in broiler to toast crust side, very lightly, turn and toast other side very lightly.

In a skillet, heat ¼ cup of olive oil and sauté onion, garlic, chopped mushrooms and tomato until done. Salt and pepper to taste. Put aside with juice.

Sauté larger remaining pieces of mushrooms in ¼ cup of hot olive oil. Cook 5 minutes on each side. Salt and pepper to taste. Place in a dish when cooked, with all the juices.

Spread sautéed onion, garlic, mushrooms and tomato onto bread then add parsley and basil. Place larger sautéed mushrooms on top with all juices. Optional: Drizzle a small amount of olive oil onto all ingredients.

Sprinkle the grated cheese on top. Broil a very, very short time, only until the cheese begins to melt.

Enjoy!

Rae Lanzilotta
Donatello Lodge #2559

MUFFALETTA

2 pizza breads in ring shape
  (found in Italian bakery)
2 (6 ounce) jars marinated
  artichoke hearts
2 (7 ounce) jars roasted red
  peppers
4½ tablespoons fresh lemon
  juice
¾ cup fresh chopped Italian
  parsley
3 teaspoons dried oregano
⅓ cup olive oil
3 cloves garlic, minced
½ teaspoon red pepper flakes
1 teaspoon dried rosemary
1 cup dry cured olives, pitted
½ pound prosciutto
½ pound provolone cheese
6 ounces salami

Day 1 (Prepare vegetable filling):
Drain artichokes, preserve liquid and chop. Drain roasted red peppers and chop. Stir artichokes, peppers, lemon juice, parsley and oregano in a medium size bowl. Cover, let stand refrigerated overnight.

Day 2 (Prepare bread/garlic paste):
Heat oil in skillet over medium heat. Add garlic and red pepper. Sauté 3 minutes until fragrant. Do not burn garlic. Remove from heat, stir in rosemary.

Slice bread horizontally. Scrape out soft bread in center. Put bread center in food processor and add garlic, pepper, oil, olives and reserved artichoke liquid. Process for one minute until it becomes like a paste.

To make sandwich: Spoon vegetables into top half of each bread where you pulled out soft center. Put layer of provolone cheese on top, then layer with salami, then with prosciutto. Spread bottom layer of each bread with prepared bread/garlic spread.

Flip bottom layers of bread onto top layers. Press firmly to compact and wrap tightly in plastic wrap. Put in refrigerator, bottom layer down, with wooden cutting board or other heavy object on top. Refrigerate at least 3 hours.

Cut into wedges and serve.

This is excellent as a light main meal or appetizer. Makes for great leftovers, the longer it is refrigerated, the better the flavor!

Regina Marie Quinn
Per Sempre Ladies Lodge #2344A

TORTA DE SPINACI

pastry shell

Filling:

3 tablespoons olive oil

1 large onion, finely chopped

2 (10 ounce) packages chopped, frozen spinach

½ cup freshly grated Parmesan cheese

1 cup (8 ounces) ricotta cheese

salt and pepper

4 eggs, lightly beaten

1 egg white

Heat oil and sauté the onion until tender but not browned. Cook spinach according to package directions; drain well. Combine drained spinach and onion and let cool. Add Parmesan cheese, ricotta cheese, salt and pepper to taste and eggs to the cooked spinach mixture.

Brush the bottom and sides of pie shell with the lightly beaten egg white. Pour in the filling. Roll out remaining pastry and cover the filling. Seal edges, make a steam hole.

Bake 40 minutes, or until the pastry is golden and done. Let stand 10 to 15 minutes before cutting (425° oven).
Yield: 8 servings.

Note: Pie can be made early in the day and reheated in a 375° oven for about 40 minutes. Cover loosely with foil to prevent over-browning.

The pie can be frozen after it has cooled, and wrapped well in aluminum foil, stored for up to two months. Allow the pie to thaw at room temperature three hours and then let it finish thawing while it is reheated in a 375° oven for about one hour.

Terrie Vanasco
Italo Balbo Lodge #2361

SPINACH BALLS I

5 eggs
2 cups Pepperidge Farm
    stuffing (in bag)
1-3 cloves garlic, chopped
2 medium onions, chopped
1 teaspoon salt

¾ cup margarine or butter,
    melted
¼ teaspoon black pepper
¾ cup Parmesan cheese
2 packages frozen chopped
    spinach, drained

Mix all above ingredients together and let sit for approximately 20 minutes. Roll into small balls and place on greased cookie sheet. Bake 15 to 20 minutes at 350°. Can be frozen.
Makes 60.

Pat DiSalvo
Donatello Lodge #2559

SPINACH BALLS II

2 cups chopped spinach,
    cooked and drained
2 tablespoons grated cheese
2 tablespoons melted butter
1½ cups bread crumbs

2 eggs
¼ cup water
⅓ teaspoon pepper
½ teaspoon salt
¼ cup olive oil

Combine spinach, cheese, butter, bread crumbs, and 1 beaten egg. Roll into balls. To the other egg, add water and seasonings and beat. Dip spinach balls into additional bread crumbs, then into egg mixture and once again in bread crumbs. Brown balls on both sides in oil.
Serves about 6.

Judith Scandiffio
Romanesque Lodge #2198

SPINACH BALLS PARMESAN

2 (10 ounce) packages frozen,
chopped spinach, cooked
according to directions and
well drained
1⅓ cups Italian style bread
crumbs
⅓ cup grated Parmesan cheese
¼ cup finely chopped celery
¼ cup finely chopped onion
½ teaspoon hot pepper sauce
¼ teaspoon nutmeg
2 eggs, lightly beaten
¼ teaspoon garlic powder

In large bowl, combine spinach, bread crumbs, cheese, celery, onion, hot pepper sauce, nutmeg and eggs; mix well. Add garlic powder and mix again. Shape spinach mixture into balls, using 1 level tablespoon per ball. In heavy 2-quart saucepan, heat 1¼ inches olive oil (approximately 3 cups) to 350°. Deep fry balls 1 minute or until golden brown. Remove with slotted spoon and drain on paper towel. Serve.

Olga V. Pacil
Geneva American Italian Lodge #2397A

ARTICHOKE PIE I

1 package frozen artichokes
3 or 4 eggs
¼ cup grated
Parmesan/Romano cheese
½ pound grated mozzarella
cheese
garlic to taste
pie crust

Boil and strain the artichokes and cut into pieces. Mix together the artichoke pieces, eggs, cheeses and garlic. Place in pie crust and bake one hour at 350°. Does not need a top crust.

Carmella Laurino
St. Francis of Assisi Lodge #2629

ARTICHOKE PIE II

1 all-purpose pie crust
1 (16 ounce) can artichoke
    hearts (in water), drain well
    and dice
1 (8 ounce) mozzarella cheese,
    (regular or skim) diced

8 ounces ricotta cheese
2 eggs
½ teaspoon pepper
¼ cup grated Parmesan cheese

Mix all of above and pour into pie shell. Bake at 325° for 30 to 40 minutes or until golden brown.
Serves 8.

Use for appetizers or lunch served with a salad.

Marilyn DiBiase
Aida Ladies Lodge #2163A

SPINACH PIE I

1 package chopped spinach
8 ounces grated mozzarella
    cheese
1 pound ricotta cheese

4 large eggs
¼ cup grated Italian cheese
1 deep dish pie shell
dash of nutmeg (if desired)

Beat eggs and add to drained spinach and rest of ingredients. Pour into pie shell and sprinkle nutmeg on top. Bake at 325° for 20 minutes and at 350° for 40 minutes.

Serve with a tossed salad.

Ann Olsen
Romanesque Lodge #2198

SPINACH PIE II

1 pound sweet Italian sausage, chopped
6 eggs
2 (10 ounce) packages frozen chopped spinach, thawed and well drained
1 (16 ounce) package mozzarella cheese, shredded

⅔ cup ricotta cheese (½ of a 16 ounce container)
½ teaspoon salt
⅛ teaspoon pepper
⅛ teaspoon garlic powder
2 tablespoons grated cheese

In a skillet, brown sausage until well browned, drain off all fat from sausage. In a large bowl combine eggs with sausage, spinach, mozzarella cheese, ricotta cheese, grated cheese, salt, pepper, and garlic powder. Pour in greased baking pan. Bake in 375° oven for about 1 hour.

Marie Castiglione
Mario Lanza Lodge #2491

ANTIPASTO PIE

8 (10-inch) flour tortillas
1 cup olive oil
20 slices Genoa salami
20 slices smoked mozzarella cheese
3 roasted red peppers, skinned and seeded

12 pieces sun-dried tomatoes (rehydrated), quartered
1 pound ricotta cheese
1 cup black olives, sliced
½ cup grated Parmesan cheese
10 slices provolone cheese
balsamic vinegar, as needed
olive oil, as needed

As you place tortillas in a 10-inch spring form pan, brush each with olive oil.

Layer as follows: tortilla; 10 pieces of salami; tortilla; 10 pieces of mozzarella; tortilla; red pepper; tortilla; black olives sprinkled with Parmesan cheese; tortilla; provolone; tortilla; salami and mozzarella; tortilla; ricotta sprinkled with sun-dried tomatoes; tortilla.

Refrigerate overnight. Remove from pan and cut into pie slices. Serve with balsamic vinegar and olive oil on the side.

Ann Bambino Lodge #2353

POTATO PIE

1 (5 pound) bag potatoes
½ pound ham, sliced and
   cut up
½ pound salami, sliced and
   cut up
1 pound mortadella, sliced and
   cut up

1 pound mozzarella cheese,
   grated
1 cup locatelli Romano cheese
1½ sticks margarine
4 eggs
½ cup milk

Peel potatoes, cut in half and boil them half way. Drain them well. Mash potatoes and add margarine, ham, salami, mozzarella, eggs (one at a time), locatelli cheese, milk and salt to taste.

Mix all together very well with your hands. Butter bottom and sides of pan and sprinkle with bread crumbs. Shake off excess. Wet your hands in milk and pour the potatoes in pan. If potatoes stick to your hands, keep working with milk. When pan is full, flatten top and sprinkle bread crumbs. Add dots of margarine all over top. Bake at 375° for 35 minutes. If you like a more golden top, put 3 to 4 minutes under the broiler. Do not bake if you are freezing. Take out frozen pie 1 hour before baking.

Enjoy!

Toni Borgese
Romanesque Lodge #2198

25

SPAGHETTI PIE I

pasta
1 cup ricotta cheese

6 ounces mozzarella cheese

Crust:
6 ounces thin spaghetti
   (vermicelli)
½ clove garlic, minced
¼ cup butter

½ cup grated Parmesan cheese
1 large egg, beaten
1 teaspoon basil, fresh or dried

Filling:
½ pound ground beef
¾ pound Italian sausage
½ cup chopped onion
1 (15 ounce) can tomato sauce
1 (6 ounce) can tomato paste

1 teaspoon sugar
1 teaspoon dried basil
1 teaspoon dried oregano
¼ cup white wine

To make crust, combine vermicelli with other crust ingredients. Chop mixture with a knife and press mixture into a 10-inch pie plate. To make filling, cook ground beef, Italian sausage (out of casing) and onion together. Drain fat. Stir in remaining ingredients. Heat throughout. To assemble pie, spread ricotta cheese on crust. Top with filling and cover with mozzarella cheese. Bake at 350° for 30 minutes.
Makes 6 to 8 servings.

George Persico
Vincent Linguanti Lodge #2212

SPAGHETTI PIE II

6 ounces spaghetti
2 tablespoons butter
½ cup grated Parmesan cheese
2 well beaten egg yolks
1 pound ground beef
½ cup chopped onion
½ cup mozzarella cheese
(shredded)

¼ cup chopped green pepper
1 (8 ounce) can tomatoes
(cut up)
1 (6 ounce) can tomato paste
1 teaspoon sugar
1 teaspoon oregano
1 clove garlic
1 cup (8 ounces) ricotta cheese

Cook spaghetti. Stir butter in hot spaghetti, add Parmesan cheese and egg yolks. Form spaghetti mixture into crust in a buttered pie plate.

In skillet cook beef, onion and green peppers until browned. Stir in undrained tomatoes, paste, sugar, oregano and garlic. Heat through. Spread ricotta cheese over spaghetti crust. Fill with tomato mixture. Bake at 350° for 20 minutes. Sprinkle shredded cheese on top and bake 5 minutes or till cheese melts.

Ann Bambino Lodge #2353

TARAMA SALADA

Italian Cracker-Bread Spread

1 jar tarama (carp roe)
1 medium onion
1 clove garlic
½ loaf bread (stale with crust
removed)

⅔ cup olive or vegetable oil
1 tablespoon dried parsley
1 teaspoon cumin powder
1 teaspoon oregano
juice of 1 lemon

Soak bread in water until soggy. Squeeze like sponge until dry but still moist. In a food processor, chop onion and garlic until fine. Add herbs, tarama, bread and oil, and puree until smooth. With machine running, very slowly add oil until incorporated. Add lemon juice. Tarama salada should thicken to consistency of heavy mayonnaise. If needed, add more oil to emulsify. Refrigerate for several hours.

Enjoy!

Cecile Marra
Le Amiche Lodge #2550

ZUCCHINI PIE I

3 cups grated zucchini (about 3
   or 4 medium zucchini)
1 onion, chopped
1 cup Bisquick
4 large eggs

¼ teaspoon salt
⅓ cup vegetable oil
½ cup grated cheese
1 teaspoon parsley
⅛ teaspoon pepper

In large mixing bowl combine all the ingredients and mix well. Grease
a 9-inch glass pie plate or spray with nonstick baking spray. Pour all
ingredients into pie plate. Bake until brown, about 40 minutes at 350°.

Anne G. Alliegro
Daughters and Sons of Italian Heritage Lodge #2428

ZUCCHINI PIE II

4 large zucchini
2 tablespoons flour
1 cup olive oil
3 tablespoons grated Parmesan
   cheese

1 cup tomato sauce
½ pound mozzarella cheese,
   sliced thin

Cut zucchini into 1-inch slices, sprinkle with flour and fry in olive oil
until light brown. In greased casserole place 1 layer of fried zucchini,
sprinkle with Parmesan cheese, a little of the sauce and cover with thin
layers of mozzarella. Repeat until all ingredients are used up, ending
with mozzarella. Bake in moderate oven (375°) for 30 minutes.
Serves 4.

Maria A. Tassone
St. Francis of Assisi Lodge #2629

ZUCCHINI LOAF

1 large zucchini, grated
1 large piece of Swiss cheese,
   grated
1 onion, grated

2 cups Bisquick
4 eggs
salt and pepper
½ cup grated cheese

Mix all together, grease loaf pan and bake for 30 to 40 minutes or until
golden brown at 375°.

Sophie Talamo
Per Sempre Ladies Lodge #2344A

IMPOSSIBLE ZUCCHINI TOMATO PIE

2 cups chopped zucchini
1 cup chopped tomato
½ cup chopped onion
⅓ cup grated Parmesan cheese
1½ cups milk

¾ cup Bisquick
3 eggs
½ teaspoon salt
¼ teaspoon pepper

Heat oven to 400°. Grease a 10-inch quiche dish or pie plate. Cut ingredients in small pieces. Sprinkle zucchini, tomato, onion and cheese in plate. Beat remaining ingredients until smooth. (1 minute with hand beater). Pour into plate. Bake until knife inserted in center comes out clean, about 30 minutes. Cool 5 minutes.

Natalie Blanco
Le Amiche Lodge #2550

ZUCCHINI CRISP

5 cups zucchini, peeled and
  sliced
½ cup lemon juice
1 teaspoon cinnamon
3 cups flour

1 cup sugar
1½ cups brown sugar
¼ teaspoon nutmeg
1 cup oleo

Cook zucchini in lemon juice until tender, add sugar, cinnamon, nutmeg, and simmer for one minute; set aside. Cut oleo into flour and brown sugar. Put half of mixture in bottom of 9 x 13-inch pan. Bake ten minutes at 375°. Pour zucchini over base crust. Add remaining ½ teaspoon cinnamon to remaining mixture and pat evenly over zucchini. Bake at 375° for 30 to 40 minutes.

Louise Moulton
Daughters of Columbus Lodge #1666

EGGPLANT ANTIPASTO

3 cups peeled and cubed
   eggplant
1 small can tomato paste
⅓ cup chopped green pepper
¼ cup water
1 chopped onion
2 tablespoons wine vinegar
¾ cup fresh sliced mushrooms

½ cup whole stuffed olives
2 cloves garlic, crushed
1½ teaspoons sugar
1 teaspoon salt
⅓ cup olive oil
½ teaspoon oregano
⅛ teaspoon pepper

Combine eggplant, green pepper, onion, mushrooms, garlic and oil in skillet. Cover and cook for 10 minutes. Add remaining ingredients. Mix and simmer until eggplant is tender, about 30 minutes.

Millie Mirabella
Donne D'Italia Lodge #2330

EGGPLANT BALLS

2 eggplants, peeled and diced
2 cups bread crumbs
3 cloves garlic or 1 teaspoon
   garlic powder
4 eggs (2 to each eggplant)

1 (8 ounce) mozzarella cheese
¼ cup parsley
½ cup Parmesan cheese
salt and pepper

Boil eggplant in salted water about 15 minutes. Place in colander to drain. Let cool. Mix all ingredients well and shape into balls. Roll in bread crumbs (additional to preceding ingredients) and fry until brown on all sides.

Gabriella Rywalt
Le Amiche Lodge #2550

MOM'S CAPONATA

3 small eggplants
1 diced onion
1 bunch celery
1 can tomato paste
1 jar capers

1 teaspoon sugar
½ cup vinegar
1 pound green olives in brine,
  crushed

Dice eggplants (unpeeled) with salt and drain overnight. Next day, sauté eggplants and diced onion till bland. Dice and cook celery for 15 minutes. To eggplants, add 1 can tomato paste plus 2 cans of water, drained capers and boiled celery. Simmer for 15 minutes. Add 1 teaspoon sugar and ½ cup vinegar. Simmer for 5 minutes. When eggplants are cold, add crushed olives.

Refrigerate.

Nancy Quinn
Per Sempre Ladies Lodge #2344A

CAPONATINA SICILIAN STYLE

4 medium eggplants
1½ cups olive oil
4 onions, sliced
½ cup tomato sauce
4 stalks celery, diced
½ cup capers

12 green olives, pitted and cut
  into pieces
1 tablespoon pine nuts
¼ cup sugar
½ cup wine vinegar
¾ teaspoon salt (optional)
½ teaspoon pepper

Peel and dice eggplants and fry in 1 cup hot olive oil. Remove fried eggplant from skillet, add remaining oil and onions and brown gently. Add tomato sauce and celery and cook until celery is tender, adding a little water if necessary. Add capers, olives, pine nuts and fried eggplant. Heat vinegar in small saucepan. Dissolve sugar in vinegar and pour over eggplant. Add salt and pepper and simmer 20 minutes, stirring frequently. Cool before serving.

This caponatina will keep a long time in refrigerator.

Frances DeSilva
Italo Balbo Lodge #2361

CAPONATA

Eggplant Appetizer

1 large eggplant (1¾ pounds)
⅔ cup and 2 tablespoons olive
   oil
1 clove garlic, minced
1 (16 ounce) can tomato puree
½ teaspoon crushed oregano
½ cup water
½ teaspoon crushed basil
¼ teaspoon pepper

1 medium onion, coarsely
   chopped
1 cup celery, sliced ¼-inch
   thick
1¼ cups pimento-stuffed
   olives, cut in halves
2 tablespoons capers, drained
1 tablespoon sugar
2 teaspoons wine vinegar
2 tablespoons minced parsley

Wash and dry eggplant then cut into 1-inch cubes. Sprinkle with salt. In a 12-inch skillet, heat ⅔ cup olive oil; add eggplant. Cook on moderate heat until brown and tender. Drain on paper towels. In the same skillet, add 2 tablespoons olive oil, onion and garlic. Stir in puree, water, oregano, basil, pepper and celery. Simmer 30 minutes, covered. Add eggplant, olives, capers, sugar, vinegar and parsley. Mix well and simmer 30 minutes, covered. Cool, cover tightly in a container and refrigerate.

Rosalie DeMarco
Aquileia Ladies Lodge #935

ARTICHOKE DIP APPETIZER

1 (14 ounce) can artichoke
   hearts, drained

1 cup mayonnaise
1 cup grated Parmesan cheese

Cut artichokes into quarters, add mayonnaise and cheese, mix and mash. Place in casserole and bake 30 minutes in a 400° oven.

Serve with crackers.

Donna Brocchi Allen
Aquileia Ladies Lodge #935

MINESTRE

SOUP

NEW YORK OSIA FILIAL LODGES

•**Binghamton Lodge #487**, Binghamton, Charter issued 1916: Originally chartered as Principe Ereditario Del Piemonte in 1916, this lodge was renamed after the city of Binghamton in Broome County. It is located in south central New York on the Susquehanna and Chenago Rivers.

•**Primavera Italica Lodge #599**, Mechanicville, Charter issued 1916: This lodge is located in an area that once was a growing industrial city where many railroads, brickyards, textile mills and paper mills drew hundreds of Italian immigrants north from New York City.

•**Columbia County Lodge #659**, Hudson, Charter issued 1982: Originally chartered in 1917 as the Loggia Cristoforo Colombo Victor Emanuel III Lodge #659, it was re-activated as the Columbia Country Lodge in 1982 to unite Italians and Italian Americans in the Hudson area.

•**Christopher Columbus Lodge #692**, Ossining, Charter issued 1917: Named after one of the greatest navigators of all times, this lodge was formed for the primary purpose of gathering Italian immigrants in Ossining together to assist each other and their families in their new found homes in America. Originally named Cristoforo Colombo, the lodge name was changed in 1978 with a new charter.

•**Aquileia Ladies Lodge #935**, White Plains, Charter issued 1919: Aquileia was one of the most important cities of the Roman Empire located on Italy's Adriatic coast near the capital of Udine. It was one of the principal naval ports and an important center of trade. Even today, the Ancient Cathedral and museum hold the largest collection of mosaic pictures and floors. This is the home lodge of our National 4th Vice President, Lucy F. Codella, who presently holds the highest office attained by a woman in the New York State Grand Lodge.

•**Loggia Glen Cove #1016**, Glen Cove, Charter issued 1920: In the early 1920's, many Italians immigrated to the Glen Cove area bringing with them old world skills as gardeners, laborers and stone masons. Many of these immigrants joined together to form the first lodge on Long Island.

•**Progresso Lodge #1047**, North Syracuse, Charter issued 1920: The name indicates "Progress" in the city of Syracuse.

•**Giovanni Da Verrazzano Lodge #1236**, Piermont, Charter issued 1923: Da Verrazzano was a Florentine explorer who entered New York Harbor in 1524, more than 85 years before Henry Hudson. The Verrazano Bridge, the longest suspension bridge in the world, is a memorial to his achievements.

•**Henry H. Rogers Lodge #1353**, Tuxedo, Charter issued 1925: Henry H. Rogers was a wealthy businessman who lived in Tuxedo Park. His gardener was an Italian gentleman who was soliciting donations for the lodge to get started. Mr. Rogers heard of their plight and donated $500.00. They were so appreciative, that the lodge was named after this generous community activist. The Order Sons of Italy in America sign on the H. H. Rogers building has been seen by millions of travelers driving on the New York State Thruway .

•**John Michael Marino Lodge #1389**, Port Washington, Charter issued 1925: The second lodge formed on Long Island is named in honor of the first Italian of the Port Washington community, a young lieutenant, who died serving his country in World War I.

(Continued on next divider page)

LENTIL SOUP

2 cups dry lentils, rinsed and
    drained
7 cups water
1 (10 ounce) package frozen
    spinach, thawed and
    drained
½ teaspoon salt
1½ cups crushed tomatoes
¼ teaspoon ground pepper

1 cup (8 ounces) tomato sauce
¼ cup olive oil
1 teaspoon Italian seasoning
1 small onion, chopped
2 cloves garlic
1 cup thinly sliced carrots
½ cup chopped celery
3 bouillon cubes
½ cup cooked rice

In a Dutch oven pan, bring lentils to a boil. Add spinach, tomatoes, tomato sauce, Italian seasoning, salt and pepper. In a large skillet, sauté onion and garlic in hot olive oil until tender. Add carrots and celery. Then add these vegetables and bouillon cubes to lentils.

Bring to a boil, lower heat. Cover and simmer for 45 minutes to 1 hour or until lentils are soft. Prepare and add rice to lentils. Stir to mix. Simmer uncovered 8 to 10 minutes.
Serves 12.

Recipe may be cut in half.

Joan Ballo
St. Francis of Assisi Lodge #2629

SPLIT PEA SOUP JARDINIERE

1 cup split peas
3 cups cold water
2 tablespoons unsalted sweet
    butter
1 cup finely chopped lean salt
    pork
2 large stalks celery, sliced
2 carrots, diced

2 tablespoons fresh parsley
1½ quarts stock or broth
1 sprig parsley
1 teaspoon thyme leaves
2 tablespoons vegetable oil
2 tablespoons all-purpose flour
1 cup heavy cream
freshly ground pepper

Combine all ingredients. Cook slowly until done to your taste.

Sarah Graziani
Constantino Brumidi Ladies Auxiliary

ESCAROLE LENTIL SOUP

1 large chopped onion
1 large clove garlic, minced
2 tablespoons minced parsley
3 tablespoons olive oil
1 pound lentils, picked over
   and rinsed (2 cups)

1 pound escarole, shredded
   coarsely (8 packed cups)
2 teaspoons salt, or to taste
½ teaspoon fresh ground
   pepper
½ cup grated Parmesan cheese

In large pot or kettle over medium heat, stir onion, garlic and parsley in oil about 5 minutes or until tender. Add 6 cups water and lentils. Bring to a boil; cover and simmer 1 hour or until lentils are tender.

Add escarole, salt and pepper; cover and simmer 10 minutes or until escarole is wilted. Add more water to desired consistency.
Makes 4 generous servings.

Serve hot in bowls, topped with Parmesan cheese. Delicious with hot garlic bread!

Gloria Ruggiero-Trofinoff
St. Francis of Assisi Lodge #2629

ZUPPA DI PESCE I

1 dozen shrimp
1 dozen mussels
1 onion, chopped
2 (10½ ounce) cans white clam
   sauce
1 dozen clams
1 lobster (optional)

5 cloves garlic, minced
1 (28 ounce) can tomato sauce
2 bottles clam juice
½ cup oil
salt, pepper and parsley to
   taste

Wash and scrub mussels and clams, clean lobster and shrimp. Let soak in cold water with a tablespoon of salt for 10 minutes, rinse and drain, put in refrigerator until sauce is ready.

Sauté onion and garlic in hot oil. Add tomato sauce, white clam sauce and clam juice. Add seasonings and cook for about ¾ of an hour on low heat. Add shrimp, clams, mussels and lobster; cook until clams and mussels open.

Dorothy Zanfardino
Romanesque Lodge #2198

ZUPPA DI PESCE II
(Fish Soup)

1 lobster, cut up	½ cup oil
12 crabs, cleaned and cut	3 cloves garlic, minced
1 dozen top neck clams	½ can Del Monte tomato sauce
1 teaspoon chopped parsley	1 teaspoon basil
¼ teaspoon oregano	1 cup dry wine

In a large pot, sauté garlic in oil until lightly brown. Add tomato sauce and cook 10 minutes at a boil. Add fish and all other ingredients. Cover pot and steam entire mixture until clams open, approximately 10 to 15 minutes. Serve over linguine or hard pepper biscuits. Garnish top with fresh parsley.

Debbie Penberg
Constantino Brumidi Ladies Auxiliary

BARLEY VEGETABLE SOUP

⅓ cup barley	1 tablespoon olive or other oil
5 cups water	1 onion, sliced
2 teaspoons salt	1 carrot, sliced
1½ cups chopped tomato	1 rib celery, sliced
1 bay leaf	2-3 cups chopped zucchini
¼ teaspoon each sage and oregano	

Bring salted water to a boil in large pot. Add barley, tomatoes, bay leaf and herbs and let simmer. Place a frying pan on medium heat and add oil. When oil is hot, add onion; stir about 1-2 minutes; add carrots and celery and stir a few minutes more; add zucchini and stir again. Reduce heat; add a bit of water and simmer for 10 to 15 minutes until liquid is almost gone. When barley has been simmering about 30 minutes, add vegetables and simmer together for 10 to 15 minutes or until vegetables are tender.
Serves 6 to 8.

Rose Frisari
William C. LaMorte Lodge #2251

BARLEY AND LENTIL SOUP

3 tablespoons of olive oil
2 medium onions, chopped
4 garlic cloves, chopped
3 carrots, chopped
4 celery stalks, chopped
1 green or red bell pepper,
    chopped
8 oil-packed sun-dried
    tomatoes, drained and
    chopped
2 teaspoons dried basil,
    crumbled
1 teaspoon dried oregano,
    crumbled

3 (14½ ounce) cans beef broth
    (may substitute beef stock
    or beef bouillon cubes
    dissolved in water)
1 (28 ounce) can crushed
    tomatoes
2 tablespoons tomato paste
1 cup barley
1 cup lentils
salt and pepper to taste
¼ cup chopped fresh parsley
    (optional)

Heat oil in heavy soup pot over medium-high heat. Sauté onions and garlic until onions are tender (about 6 minutes). Add next 6 ingredients. Cook until bell pepper softens, stir occasionally.

Mix in broth and water, tomatoes and tomato paste. Bring to a boil, stir in lentils and barley. Reduce heat, simmer about 1½ to 1¾ hours. Stir occasionally. Note that barley may absorb liquid after 1 hour. Add additional water or beef broth if needed. Beef broth gives better flavor.

Season with salt and pepper. Ladle into bowls and garnish with parsley, if desired.
Serves 8.

Russ Romano
Judge Frank A. Gulotta Lodge #2180

ZUPPA DI COZZE ALLA TARANTINA

(Taranto Mussel Soup/Stew)

3-3½ quarts mussels
¼ cup olive oil
2 cloves garlic
¼ of a hot chili pepper
1 pound ripe tomatoes
   or ¼ cup tomato paste

1 cup dry white wine
   (optional)
salt and pepper
slices of toasted bread

Scrape the mussels with stiff brush and remove their beards. Wash them particularly carefully until no trace of sand remains. Heat the oil in a large pan and sauté 1 clove of garlic, lightly crushed, and the piece of chili pepper until browned. Discard both and add tomatoes, peeled, seeded and chopped, or the tomato paste diluted in water. Cook over a brisk heat for 10 minutes, then drop in mussels. Cover and cook until the mussels open, shaking the pan occasionally. Stir well, add wine, if used, and cook briskly until reduced. Sprinkle with remaining garlic, finely chopped. The soup may be served as it is with slices of toasted bread, or the mussels may first be scooped out of shells and returned to pan.
Serves 6.

Lorraine Gargiulo
Le Amiche Lodge #2550

MERLUZZO

(Fish Soup)

2 pounds whiting
1 or 2 cloves garlic, chopped
2 tablespoons chopped parsley

3 tablespoons olive oil
4 cups warm water
salt and pepper to taste

In a saucepan, cook parsley and garlic in olive oil until garlic is soft. Add warm water and bring to a boil. Add fish, salt and pepper. Cover and simmer for 10 minutes. Remove fish, discard bones. Serve broth and fish with small cooked pasta.
Serves 4.

Veronica Martino
William C. LaMorte Lodge #2251

ZUPPA DI CLAMS AND MUSSELS

3 dozen clams, unshelled
3 dozen mussels, unshelled
4 cups clam juice
3 cups canned tomato puree
6 tablespoons olive oil

3-4 cloves garlic, minced
1 teaspoon oregano
2 tablespoons parsley, minced
salt and white pepper to taste

Wash and scrub shellfish well. In a large pot, sauté garlic and oil. Add the shellfish, clam juice and tomatoes. Season to taste with salt and pepper. Add oregano and parsley. Cover and cook over low heat until the shells open.

With a large spoon, serve into bowls. Have some crusty, seeded Italian bread and enjoy!
Serves 6.

Any leftover sauce can be used on top of cooked linguine.

GiGi Manzella
Dr. Vincenzo Sellaro Lodge #2319

AVGOLEMONO

(Chicken Soup with Egg and Lemon)

1 whole chicken
6-8 cups broth
1 cup rice

3 eggs, separated
1 lemon (only juice)
salt and pepper

Boil chicken until cooked. Remove chicken. Boil broth with 1 cup of rice. When rice is cooked, lower heat to simmer.

In a mixing bowl, put 3 egg whites and beat until stiff, then add egg yolks and blend into egg whites with a beater. Add lemon juice slowly while beating, then add broth a little at a time, slowly, until all broth has been used. Beat well. Pour this mixture into pot, stirring well. Pieces of chicken may now be added to soup if desired.

Mary Lynn Kermidas
Daughters of Columbus Lodge #1666

SICILIAN SAUSAGE SOUP

½ pound bulk pork sausage or
    Italian sweet sausage
1 cup chopped onion
1 (2 pound, 3 ounce) can Italian
    tomatoes
2 (13¾ ounce) cans (or 3½ cups)
    chicken broth

1 teaspoon basil leaf, crushed
½ cup orzo (rice-shaped)
    macaroni
¼ teaspoon salt
⅛ teaspoon pepper

Cook sausage in large saucepan, breaking up meat with wooden spoon until all pink color has disappeared. (If using Italian sausage, remove casing before cooking.) Sauté onions in pan until soft.

Add tomatoes (if whole, crush before adding). Add broth and basil. Bring to a boil. Stir in orzo, salt and pepper. Lower heat and simmer 20 minutes until orzo is tender.

Taste and add additional salt and pepper if desired.
Serves 4.

Ruby Vitelli
Aida Ladies Lodge #2163A

EGG DROP SOUP

1 quart chicken broth or
    bouillon
2 eggs
⅛ teaspoon salt

1½ tablespoons semolina
2 tablespoons grated Parmesan
    cheese

Combine eggs, salt, semolina, cheese and 3 tablespoons cool broth in mixing bowl and beat with fork 5 minutes. Bring rest of broth to boiling point and add egg mixture slowly, stirring constantly. Continue stirring while soup simmers 5 minutes.
Serves 4.

Vito Saliani
Rockland Lodge #2176

STRACCIATELLA ALLA ROMANA

(Chicken Egg Drop Soup)

4 cups chicken broth
2 eggs
1 teaspoon chopped parsley

2 tablespoons grated cheese
pinch of nutmeg
salt to taste

Beat together eggs, cheese and spices. Bring chicken broth to boiling point and add cheese mixture. Boil for 1 minute, breaking up egg and cheese mixture with fork.
Serves 4.

Josephine Baldanza
Romanesque Lodge #2198

MINESTRONE MILAN STYLE

1 teaspoon olive oil
⅛ pound pork, chopped
½ clove garlic
½ medium size onion, chopped
1 teaspoon chopped parsley
1 teaspoon chopped sage
1 teaspoon salt
½ teaspoon pepper
1 tablespoon tomato paste
3 stalks celery, chopped

2 carrots, sliced
2 potatoes, diced
2 cups cooked peas
¼ small cabbage, shredded
2 zucchini, diced
1½ quarts water or stock
1 cup elbow macaroni
4 tablespoons grated Romano
   cheese

Place olive oil in a large soup pot, add salt, pork, garlic, onion, parsley, sage and pepper and brown a little. Add tomato paste diluted in 1 cup water. Cook 5 minutes. Add all vegetables, water or stock and cook slowly for 45 minutes. Add elbow macaroni and cook 10 minutes longer. Place in bowls and sprinkle with cheese.
Serves 6.

Maria A. Tassone
St. Francis of Assisi Lodge #2629

MINESTRA MARITITTA

A Marriage of Greens and Meat

1 head of escarole	1 head of chicory
1 head of white cabbage	1 head of red cabbage

Simmer greens together for 35 minutes.

1 pork loin, about 1 or 1½ pounds	1 ham end
1 piece prosciutto, ½ pound	1 salami, about 1 pound piece

Simmer meats together for approximately 1½ hours. Drain water from greens and add to meats. Cool all together for 35 minutes and serve hot.

Millie Alessi
Dr. Vincenzo Sellaro Lodge #2319

TOMATO SOUP JUSTINA

1 onion	4 cups chicken stock
2 pounds skinned and seeded tomatoes, chopped	salt and pepper
1 garlic clove	pinch of sugar
1 tablespoon fresh chopped basil	1 cup cooked rice

Sauté onion and tomatoes. Add garlic clove and basil. Cook 5 minutes. Add stock. Puree in blender or processor. Return to pan and cook another 5 minutes. Add cooked rice at the end. Salt and pepper to taste. Serve with hot crostini of cheese or anchovy.

Lucy Castagna
Italian Heritage Lodge #2227

MINESTRONE SOUP I

1 can white beans
½ can chick peas
1 cup carrots, diced
1 cup turnip, diced
1½ cups cabbage, shredded
1 cup string beans
1 cup peas
3 stalks celery, chopped
2½ quarts water
3 teaspoons salt
½ teaspoon pepper

pinch oregano
2 tablespoons butter or
   margarine
2 slices bacon, minced
1 large onion, chopped
½ cup parsley, optional
1 (16 ounce) can tomatoes,
   chopped
1 clove garlic, sliced in half
½ pound spaghetti, broken in
   small pieces

In water, add white beans, chick peas, carrots, turnip, cabbage, string beans and peas. Stir and add salt, pepper and oregano. Bring to boil and simmer, uncovered, for 30 minutes.

In a fry pan, melt butter or margarine, minced bacon and onion. Sauté until soft. Add parsley, tomatoes, celery and garlic. Simmer for 5 minutes and add to broth.

Continue cooking on low heat (covered) for 1 to 1½ hours or until vegetables are soft. Boil broken spaghetti, drain and add to minestrone. Serve with garlic bread.
Yield: 10 to 12 hearty servings.

Michael Bologna
Mario Lanza Lodge #2491

QUICK PASTA BROCCOLI SOUP

1 large onion, chopped
1 garlic clove, minced
2 tablespoons butter or
   margarine

6 cups water
3 chicken bouillon cubes
1 cup orzo
1 bunch fresh broccoli, cut

Cook and stir onion in hot butter until tender but not browned. Add water and bouillon cubes and bring to a boil. Stir in pasta, simmer 5 minutes. Add broccoli and simmer 5 minutes longer.
Makes 8 servings.

Phil Politi
Rockland Lodge #2176

MINESTRONE SOUP II

1 cup macaroni
1 teaspoon oil
3 slices chopped bacon
½ chopped onion
chopped parsley
salt and pepper

1 tablespoon tomato paste
3 stalks celery, diced
2 carrots, diced
2 potatoes, diced
2 cups cooked beans
1½ quarts water

In a large soup pan, sauté bacon, garlic, onion, parsley, salt and pepper. Add tomato paste diluted in 1 cup water. Cook 5 minutes then add all vegetables and water. Boil gently 45 minutes. Add macaroni and cook till tender. Sprinkle soup with grated cheese.
Serves 6.

Judith Molina
Italian Heritage Lodge #2227

ITALIAN BEAN SOUP

1 cup dry navy beans
1 teaspoon salt
1 (8 ounce) can tomato sauce
1 cup chopped onion
1 cup chopped carrots
½ cup chopped green pepper

2 cloves garlic, minced
2 beef bouillon cubes
1 teaspoon sweet basil
1 teaspoon oregano
½ cup macaroni, uncooked

Rinse beans, add 8 cups water. Soak overnight. Do not drain. Stir in salt and remaining ingredients except macaroni. Cover and simmer 1½ to 2 hours. Stir in macaroni and cook, uncovered, until macaroni is done, about 15 minutes.
Serves 8.

Nancy Boushie
Stella D'Argento Lodge #1916

HEARTY TORTELLINI SOUP

2 crushed garlic cloves
1 tablespoon margarine
3 cans (13¾ ounce) College Inn
  Chicken Broth
1 pound cheese tortellini

1 (10 ounce) package chopped
  spinach, thawed or 1 head
  of escarole
1 (16 ounce) can stewed
  tomatoes, undrained
grated cheese

In a large saucepan, over medium high heat, cook garlic in margarine for 2 to 3 minutes. Add broth and tortellini, heat to a boil. Reduce heat, simmer 10 minutes. Add spinach (or escarole) and tomatoes; simmer 5 minutes more. Serve topped with cheese.
Makes 6 servings.

Bon Appetit!

Maria Rossiello
Anthony Casamento Lodge #2612

PANE E PIZZE

BREAD AND PIZZA

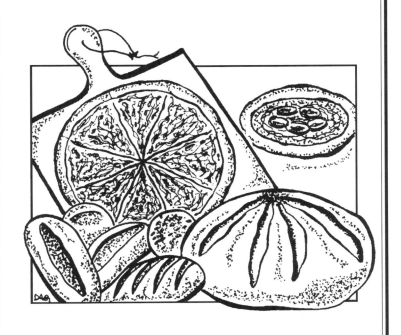

NEW YORK OSIA FILIAL LODGES

• **San Rocco Lodge #1623**, Cortland, Charter issued 1932: This lodge was named after San Rocco, who was born in France and canonized for miracles in northern Italy. He was widely revered among southern Italians for his cures of the diseased and maimed.

• **Daughters of Columbus Lodge #1666**, Endicott, Charter issued 1933: This lodge was first instituted as the "Marie Jose Di Savoia" Lodge, whose namesake was the last Italian princess. The name was later changed because it sounded more American and lessened the concern of negative attitudes towards Italians at that time in our history. This lodge is presently the largest women's lodge in the State of New York.

• **Stella D'Oro Lodge #1730**, Cortland, Charter issued 1934: Named as the Golden Star of the city of Cortland.

• **Stella D'Argento Lodge #1916**, Binghamton, Charter issued 1941: This women's lodge was first established under the name of Silver Star Lodge and the name was later changed to reflect the Italian ancestry Stella D'Argento.

• **Italian American Women's Lodge #1979**, Corning, Charter issued 1948: This lodge was first organized as the Italian-American Women's Club of Corning and in 1948 became part of the Order.

• **Va Pensiero Lodge #1994**, Dobbs Ferry, Charter issued 1949: The name Va Pensiero means "Go with my thoughts" and was chosen from Giuseppe Verdi's opera "Nabucco". The opera was set around the time of the Revolution in Italy.

• **Utica Lodge #2054**, Utica, Charter issued 1956: This lodge was sponsored in its formation by the Adelaide Caroili Society, an Italian-American woman's organization formed in 1917.

• **Mount Vernon Lodge #2089**, Mount Vernon, Charter issued 1959: Named after the city of Mount Vernon in southern Westchester County.

• **Vincent Lombardi Lodge #2091**, The Bronx, Charter issued in 1959: Vincent Lombardi signed on as head coach and general manager of the Green Bay Packers in 1959. He went on to accumulate an astounding six conference titles and two NFL championships in nine years. He was inducted into the Football Hall of Fame in 1971.

• **American Daughter's Lodge #2092**, The Bronx, Charter issued 1959.

• **Arturo Toscanini Lodge #2107**, Huntington, Charter issued 1960: This was the first lodge chartered in Suffolk County. Permission to use the name of Arturo Toscanini was granted by his son Walter. "The Maestro" was a child prodigy who conducted "Aida" in Rio de Janeiro at the age of nineteen from memory. He went on to become the conductor of Milan's La Scala and New York's Philharmonic and NBC Orchestras. This is the home lodge of National Immediate Past President, Peter R. Zuzolo, who was the first New Yorker elected to that esteemed position in over 50 years and served from 1991-1993.

• **Fanfani Ladies Lodge #2128A**, The Bronx, Charter issued 1964: Amintore Fanfani was the former premier of Italy, who is a lifetime member of the Italian Senate, former President of the General Assembly of the United Nations, a professor of economic history and a painter.

• **Santa Rosalia Lodge #2131**, The Bronx, Charter issued 1963 as the Giuseppe Fusco Lodge; St. Rosalia is the patron Saint of Sicily. Rosalia was a daughter of a noble family from Palermo. She spent her life completely dedicated to God and died in a cave on Monte Pellegrino.

(Continued on next divider page)

ITALIAN PIZZA BREAD

1 package crescent rolls
¼ pound provolone cheese,
  sliced thin

¼ pound salami, sliced thin
roasted peppers

Lay crescent rolls down and press into 1-inch long sheet. Layer in center, provolone cheese, salami and top with roasted peppers. Pull sides up and pinch together all seams. Turn over (gently) and bake until slightly golden brown, approximately 30 minutes.
Serves 6.

Maria A. Tassone
St. Francis of Assisi Lodge #2629

BELLA NANA'S BREAD PIE

2 cups seasoned bread crumbs
3 eggs, beaten
1 small onion, chopped
1 clove garlic, chopped
1 tablespoon parsley, fresh if
  possible

¼ cup grated Italian cheese
1 cup milk
salt and pepper to taste
¼ cup olive oil

Mix together all above ingredients except for olive oil. Mixture should be thicker than a cake batter; if too thick, add milk.

Heat olive oil in 10-inch fry pan. Pour mixture into fry pan and smooth out like a large pancake. Keep heat at medium temperature. Cook pie for about 10 minutes and lightly brown on one side, flip over on other side and cook an additional 10 minutes.
Serves 6 to 8 people.

Served as a side dish, especially "Monday Soup Night."

Rita Panico
Jane H. Landi Lodge #2239A

PEPPERONI BREAD

1 pound frozen bread dough, thawed
½ cup chopped onion
2 tablespoons butter or margarine

1 cup mozzarella cheese, cut in strips
¼ pound domestic pepperoni
1 beaten egg
poppy or sesame seeds

In a small skillet, cook onion in butter or margarine until tender.

On floured surface, roll out bread dough to a 17 x 7-inch rectangle. Spread cooked onion evenly over dough. Sprinkle cheese and pepperoni on top. Roll up jelly-roll style from the long side, pinching edges to seal. Place roll seam side down on greased cookie sheet. Score top of loaf crosswise, making cuts ¼-inch deep.

Cover. Let rise in a warm place 45 to 60 minutes or until almost doubled.

Brush top of bread with egg. Sprinkle with seeds. Bake in 350° oven for 25 to 30 minutes.

Rosalie Wyer
Verrazano Lodge #212

SAUSAGE BREAD

2 pizza dough (1 pound each)
1½ pounds mozzarella cheese, shredded
2 pounds Italian sausage
parsley flakes

Parmesan cheese
sesame seed (optional)
Accent
garlic powder
1 egg

Place dough in a greased bowl and cover (let rise). Remove sausage from casing and fry; add seasonings to taste. Drain.

Flatten dough to ½-inch thickness. Spread out sausage on top. Spread out mozzarella on top of sausage. Roll dough (jelly-roll style), squeeze ends together. Place on greased cookie sheet. Beat egg and baste on dough. Sprinkle with sesame seeds if desired. Bake in 375° oven for 35 to 40 minutes, until golden brown.

Donna Petrucci
Donne D'Italia Lodge #2330

SPINACH ROLL BREAD

1 pound pizza or bread dough
1 box frozen spinach
a little oil and garlic
¼ cup grated
    Parmesan/Romano cheese
½ cup grated mozzarella cheese

Roll out dough.

Cook and strain spinach. Fry spinach in a little oil and garlic. Cool. Mix in the cheeses and spread mixture on dough. Roll like a jelly roll, ending with seam-side down on bottom. Brush with white of egg and prick the dough.

Bake at 350° until brown. May take ½ to 1 hour.

Carmella Laurino
St. Francis of Assisi Lodge #2629

ZUCCHINI BREAD I

3 eggs
1½ cups sugar
2 cups sifted all-purpose flour
1 teaspoon baking soda
1 teaspoon baking powder
1 teaspoon salt
1 cup chopped walnuts
1 cup vegetable oil
2 cups zucchini, grated
3 teaspoons ground cinnamon
1 cup raisins
2 teaspoons vanilla

Beat eggs lightly in a large bowl. Stir in oil, sugar, zucchini and vanilla. Sift flour, baking powder, baking soda, cinnamon and salt. Stir into egg mixture until well blended. Stir in nuts and raisins. Spoon batter into 2 well-buttered 8 x 5 x 3-inch loaf pans.

Bake in moderate oven at 375° for 1 hour or until center springs back when lightly pressed with fingertips or a toothpick stuck in the center comes out clean. Cool in pan on wire rack for 10 minutes. Remove from pans and cool completely. Can also be frozen. Great with cream cheese.

Paul W. Ludwig, Jr.
Vincent Linguanti Lodge #2212

ZUCCHINI BREAD II

1 package yellow cake mix
3 eggs
½ cup butter or margarine,
    softened
½ cup water

½ teaspoon ground cinnamon
2 cups grated zucchini
½ cup chopped walnuts
confectioners sugar (optional)

Preheat oven to 375°; grease 13 x 9 x 2-inch pan. Combine cake mix, eggs, butter, water and cinnamon in large bowl. Beat at low speed with electric mixer until moistened. Beat at medium speed for 4 minutes. Stir in zucchini. Pour into pan; sprinkle with walnuts. Bake at 375° for 30 to 35 minutes or until toothpick inserted in center comes out clean. Dust with confectioners sugar if desired.
Makes 12 to 16 servings.

Bea Acorn
St. Thomas Aquinas Lodge #2569

ZUCCHINI LOAF

3 cups thin-sliced, peeled
    zucchini
2 cups Bisquick
1 cup chopped onion
½ cup grated cheese
½ teaspoon oregano

parsley
dash of pepper
½ teaspoon salt
1 clove garlic, chopped
½ cup oil
4 eggs, beaten

Mix all together; add zucchini last. Bake at 350° in a loaf pan until golden brown.

Rose Carozzoni
Italian American Women's Lodge #1979

CHOCOLATE ZUCCHINI BREAD

3 eggs
3 cups flour
1 cup oil
2 cups sugar
¼ teaspoon baking powder
1 teaspoon baking soda
1 teaspoon vanilla
2 cups grated zucchini

1 teaspoon salt
1 teaspoon cinnamon
1 cup nuts (optional)
2 ounces unsweetened Baker's chocolate or 6 tablespoons cocoa
2 tablespoons oil

In a large bowl beat eggs; beat in sugar and oil. Melt chocolate; add to mixture. Add zucchini and vanilla. Stir dry ingredients into mixture. Add nuts and mix well. Grease two 5 x 9-inch loaf pans. Pour in batter. Bake at 350° for 50 to 60 minutes. Cool in pan 15 minutes before removing. Bread freezes well.

Peggy Fratto
Raffaello Lodge #2661

APPLE BREAD

3 cups finely chopped apples (any variety)
2 cups sugar
3 cups flour
1 teaspoon cinnamon
1 teaspoon vanilla
1 teaspoon salt
3 eggs, beaten

1 teaspoon baking soda
½ cup softened butter or margarine
1 cup raisins, plumped in cold water and drained
1 cup chopped walnuts (optional)

Mix all together the apples, sugar, flour, cinnamon, vanilla, salt and baking soda. Cream the softened butter into the mixture. Beat 3 eggs and add. Pour batter into two greased 5 x 9-inch loaf pans. Add raisins and nuts. Bake at 350° for 1 hour. Cool in pans before removing.

Peggy Fratto
Raffaello Lodge #2661

BANANA NUT BREAD

2½ cups flour
1 cup sugar
3½ teaspoons baking powder
1 teaspoon salt
3 tablespoons oil

¾ cup milk
1 egg
1 cup mashed ripe bananas
1 cup chopped walnuts

Mix dry ingredients; add oil/milk/egg mixture and mashed bananas. Fold in walnuts and place in greased and floured loaf pan. Bake at 350° for 55 to 65 minutes.

Kay Ward
Guy Lombardo Lodge #2417

GRANDMA MISURACA'S BREAD

7 cups flour
1 egg
1 envelope yeast
3 cups bulgur wheat (soaked
    until soft)

sesame seeds
½ stick butter (melted)
1 tablespoon honey
1 tablespoon salt

Mix flour and salt in large mixing bowl. Stir in melted butter. Mix yeast and honey in 1 cup of lukewarm water.

Make 2 indentations in flour and add the egg in one, and the yeast mixture into the other. Mix ingredients and add bulgur wheat. Continue to add lukewarm water until dough is moist but not too watery.

Leave in bowl, covered with a clean cloth until it doubles in size.

Beat down the dough and make the sign of the cross over it. Then cut off fist sized pieces to make rolls, or put dough in bread pans for loaves.

Cover with sesame seeds and let rise until doubled in size again.

Bake at 450° for 30 minutes or until brown.

Best served hot with olive oil.

Marc J. Randazza

LEMON BREAD

¾ stick butter or margarine
1 cup sugar
2 eggs
¼ cup milk
1½ cups flour

1 teaspoon baking powder
½ teaspoon salt
½ cup chopped nuts
grated rind of 1 lemon

Mix and bake at 350° in a small loaf pan. Remove from oven, but leave in pan. When bread goes into oven, mix juice of lemon and ½ cup sugar. When out of oven, pour juice and sugar mixture over bread and let soak in before removing from pan.

Jo Seidel
America Lodge #2245

NIGHT-BEFORE FRENCH TOAST WITH ITALIAN BREAD

1 (10 ounce) long, thin Italian
    bread or French bread loaf
8 large eggs
3 cups milk
4 teaspoons sugar

¾ teaspoon salt
1 tablespoon vanilla
2 tablespoons lightly salted
    butter or margarine, cut up
    in small pieces

Butter a 9 x 13-inch pan. Cut bread into 1-inch thick slices and arrange in single layer in pan. In large bowl, beat eggs with remaining ingredients except butter. When thoroughly mixed, pour over bread in pan. Cover with foil and refrigerate from 4 to 36 hours.

To bake, uncover pan, dot with butter, put in oven. Turn oven on to 350° and bake 45 to 50 minutes until bread is puffy and lightly browned. Remove and let stand 5 minutes before serving.
Makes 8 servings.

Serve with choice of syrup, honey, yogurt or sour cream and fresh fruit.

Grace Moretti Eagan
Giouse Carducci Lodge #226A

PIZZA CARCIOFI

Dough:

2¾ cups bread flour
1 teaspoon salt
1 teaspoon active dried yeast
  (fast rising)

1 teaspoon sugar
about ¾ cup warm water
1 tablespoon olive oil

Combine yeast, sugar and ¼ cup water in a small bowl; leave until frothy. Add this mixture to flour in a medium bowl with remaining water, oil and salt. Mix to a soft dough; knead on a floured surface for about 10 minutes or until smooth. Place in a warm area and let rise for 45 minutes or until doubled in size. Punch down risen dough on a 12-inch pizza pan. Pinch up edges to make a rim.

Sauce:

1 (16 ounce) can crushed
  tomatoes
2 tablespoons olive oil
1 finely chopped onion
1 tablespoon chopped fresh
  basil

1 tablespoon tomato paste
½ teaspoon sugar
1 clove garlic, chopped
salt and pepper to taste

Heat oil in saucepan. Add onion and garlic; cook until soft. Stir in tomatoes, tomato paste, sugar and basil. Season to taste with salt and pepper. Cover and simmer until thick.

Topping:

½ cup shredded Fontina cheese
8 sun-dried tomatoes in oil

6 ounces artichoke hearts
  (marinated)

Spread desired amount of sauce on pizza dough. Sprinkle with cheese. Drain artichokes, saving oil. Arrange artichokes on pizza. Chop sun-dried tomatoes. Sprinkle over artichokes. Salt and pepper to taste. Sprinkle with 1 or 2 tablespoons of artichoke oil. Bake 20 minutes or until dough is golden.
Makes 2 servings.

Angelo Angerame
Raffaello Lodge #2661

PIZZA RUSTICA I

1 pound bread dough
2 pounds ricotta cheese
6 eggs
1 teaspoon black pepper
1 cup chopped parsley

½ cup grated cheese
1 pound basket cheese
½ pound prosciutto
½ pound soppressato
½ pound capocollo

Separate dough in two parts, half for bottom crust and half for top. Chop all the meats and basket cheese. Mix ricotta and eggs well. Add pepper, grated cheese, parsley and chopped ingredients. Mix well. Pour into dough-lined pan. Cover with the rest of the dough. Roll edges of dough together to avoid spillover. Brush top with egg white (optional).

Bake at 350° until firm and golden brown.

Jean Rivieccio
Per Sempre Ladies Lodge #2344A

PIZZA RUSTICA II

Crust:

3 cups flour
¾ cup softened butter
salt

2 eggs, lightly beaten
ice water

Filling:

1 pound ricotta cheese
⅓ pound diced provolone
   cheese
½ pound diced mozzarella
   cheese
1⅔ cups grated cheese

4 eggs, lightly beaten
¼ pound salami (or dry
   sausage)
2-3 sprigs parsley, finely
   chopped
salt and pepper to taste

1 egg, beaten, to brush pastry

Sift flour on board or into bowl and rub in the butter. Add pinch of salt and eggs. Work quickly, just enough to mix ingredients into a dough. Add ice water, a tablespoon at a time to make dough, keep mixing with fork. Put aside in floured bowl, and leave covered for ½ hour.

Mix 4 cheeses in bowl and add eggs, salami, parsley and pinch of salt and pepper. Put aside.

Divide dough into 2 pieces, one slightly larger than the other. Roll into sheets. Line with layer. Spread filling and cover with remaining sheet. Head edges. This is enough for 12-inch pie. Pinch all over with fork. Brush with beaten egg.

Bake 1 hour at 375° until top is golden brown.

Jean Miraglia
Daughters and Sons of Italian Heritage Lodge #2428

PIZZA RUSTICA III

(Carnival Pie)

1 pound ricotta cheese
2 raw eggs
2 hard boiled eggs (sliced)
4 ounces provolone cheese
2 ounces salami

4 ounces ham
6-8 ounces mozzarella cheese
2 ounces pepperoni
2 tablespoons grated cheese

Make an 8- or 9-inch two-crust pie or buy frozen pie shells.

Cut all ingredients in strips, slice hard boiled eggs. Combine ricotta cheese, raw eggs and grated cheese and beat. Mix all ingredients together and pour into pie crust. Cover with top crust and brush with egg yolk or whole egg. If using frozen shell it will need to be molded. Cover pie edges with foil so it doesn't burn and bake in 375° oven until brown, 45 minutes to 1 hour.

Can be served hot, cold or lukewarm.

Pastry crust:
2 cups flour
¾ cup Crisco shortening

1 teaspoon salt
6-8 tablespoons cold water

Mix all ingredients, cut Crisco into pea size and mix with hands until it holds together. If more water is needed, add a spoonful at a time. Divide in half and roll out on pastry cloth and line pie pan.

Pauline Nocella
Italo Balbo Lodge #2361

LA FOCACCIA

Dough:
2 medium potatoes, mashed
    and lukewarm
7 cups flour
1 package yeast

1 cup lukewarm water
2 tablespoons olive oil
2 tablespoons salt

Topping:
½ (32 ounce) can whole
    tomatoes
oregano
black pepper

garlic powder (optional)
4 ounces mozzarella cheese,
    sliced thin

To mix by hand: Dissolve yeast in lukewarm water. Measure flour onto large wooden board, making a well in the center of flour. Pour in yeast mixture. Add mashed potatoes, olive oil and salt. Knead until a large ball forms. If too sticky, add more flour.

Rise in warm place in a covered pot or bowl (lightly greased with oil) for 5 hours.

Knead again slightly. Stretch dough to fit 11 x 15-inch oiled baking pan. Cover tightly with foil; rise one more hour. Make indentations in dough with fingers. Crush tomatoes into indentations. Pour liquid over top. Sprinkle with oregano, black pepper and garlic powder. Bake in 350° oven until golden brown (about 50 minutes).

Slice mozzarella thin over focaccia. Bake 10 minutes more, or until cheese melts. Serve warm or hot.

Using food processor (to mix dough): Follow same steps, using processor instead of board, but mix only half of the ingredients at a time, as processor (which kneads) only holds 3½ cups flour.
Makes 8 to 10 servings.

This recipe comes from the village of Palo del Colle, Bari.

Angelina Spero
Cellini Lodge #2206

Pasta e Riso

Pasta and Rice

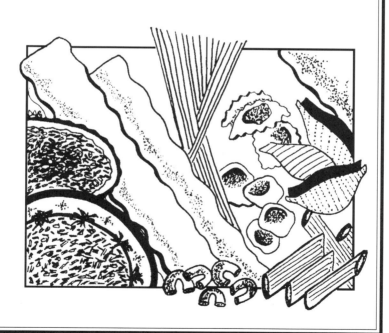

NEW YORK OSIA FILIAL LODGES

•**Renaissance Lodge #2139**, The Bronx, Charter issued 1963: The Renaissance was a time of great renewal of art, literature and learning in Europe beginning with the 14th century and extending into the 17th century.

•**LaGuardia Queens Lodge #2141**, Richmond Hill, Charter issued 1963: Fiorello LaGuardia was the first Italian-American elected as Mayor of the City of New York. The colorful "Little Flower" was admired for his honesty, courage and toughness in City government.

•**Columbus Lodge #2143**, South Farmingdale, Charter issued 1963: Christopher Columbus landed in the New World on that fateful morning of October 12, 1492. The Genoese navigator, sailing under the flag of Spain, changed the course of human events, beginning a 500 year history of Italian contributions to the greatness of America.

•**Enrico Fermi Lodge #2150**, Freeport, Charter issued 1965: This famous physicist was born in Italy in 1901. In 1938, he received the Nobel Prize in Physics for work on radioactive substance. He worked on the atomic bomb project and created the first self-sustaining chain reaction in uranium.

•**Giuseppe Verdi Lodge #2163**, Woodbury, Charter issued 1965: Giuseppe Verdi is known as one of the greatest writers and composers of opera. He produced and presented the famous operas "Rigoletto, "Aida" and "Falstaff".

•**Aida Ladies Lodge #2163A**, Woodbury, Charter issued 1968: "Aida" was one of Giuseppe Verdi's greatest grand operas. Verdi was commissioned by the King of Egypt to write this opera. This was the first women's lodge formed in Nassau County.

•**Rockland Lodge #2176**, Blauvelt, Charter issued 1966: This lodge enjoys the distinction of being the largest lodge in the county of Rockland. Its name was derived from the area in which its members reside.

•**Judge Frank A. Gulotta Lodge #2180**, Lynbrook, Charter issued 1960: Chartered as the Unitals Lodge, the name was changed in 1990 to honor Frank A. Gulotta who was the first Italian American elected to the office of Nassau County District Attorney. He later became a Judge and his son, Thomas S. Gulotta, is currently the Nassau County Executive.

•**William Paca Lodge #2189**, West Babylon, Charter issued 1967: In 1776, William Paca of Maryland, was the 37th signer of the Declaration of Independence. Later he became the governor and Chief Justice of the State.

•**Romanesque Lodge #2198**, Blauvelt, Charter issued 1968: The name Romanesque was derived from the exquisite Roman architectural design that was developed in Italy during the Roman Empire.

•**Andrea Doria Lodge #2201**, Selden, Charter issued 1968: Andrea Doria was a Genoese admiral and statesman. He fought in the French service in Italian Wars until 1528 and later fought for Emperor Charles V.

(Continued on next divider page)

PESTO A LA GRAND LODGE

4 cups basil leaves, washed
  and air-dried or spin-dried
2 cups fresh parsley, curly style
  preferred

¼ cup pignoli nuts, almonds or
  walnuts, chopped
4 large cloves garlic, chopped
1 cup Parmesan cheese

In a large bowl add basil leaves to parsley after chopping each in blender or food processor. Add nuts and garlic. Mix in Parmesan cheese or shake all ingredients once bowl is covered. Do not add any oil; keep mixture dry in small plastic container and use over fresh cooked pasta, al dente.

Boil pasta, drain, saving ½ cup of liquid. Add stick of margarine or ½ cup of liquid from cooked pasta. No oil or butter — keep it light.

Mangia!
Serves 8.

Joseph Sciame
State President
Grand Lodge of New York
Member of Cellini Lodge #2206

PESTO A LA PIZZOLATO

2 cups fresh basil leaves,
  tightly packed
3-5 cloves garlic
1-2 tablespoons pine nuts

approximately ¼ cup good
  olive oil
2 cups fresh peeled tomatoes

Pour olive oil into blender; add nuts and garlic; then add basil leaves. Remove when all is pureed. Pour into a large serving bowl and add cut up fresh tomatoes and their juice. Tomatoes must not be cooked. Serve over al dente noodles of your choice.

Veronica Martino
William C. LaMorte Lodge #2251

PUTTANESCA SAUCE

1 small onion, chopped
ham chunks, optional
½ large green pepper
3 tablespoons olive oil
4 cloves garlic, crushed

basil, oregano and parsley
salt and pepper to taste
6-8 cut up tomatoes
1 bunch of broccoli
1 can pitted black olives, sliced

In a large saucepan, brown olive oil, onion, ham and green pepper. Add garlic and brown lightly. Add basil, oregano, parsley and salt and pepper to taste.

Add tomatoes and simmer for approximately 15 minutes. Add al dente cooked broccoli and black olives. Cook sauce an additional 5 minutes and serve over any pasta.
Serves 6 people.

Donna Addeo
Jane H. Landi Lodge #2239A

ROSE'S "DOCTORED" TOMATO SAUCE

2 tablespoons butter
1 medium onion, chopped
3 cloves garlic, minced
½ green bell pepper, chopped
1 teaspoon dried Italian
    seasoning

¼ cup red wine
freshly ground pepper to taste
1 (32 ounce) jar traditional-
    flavor spaghetti sauce

Heat butter in a medium-size saucepan over low heat. Add onions, garlic and green pepper and sauté for about 10 minutes, until soft. Add remaining ingredients and simmer for about 20 minutes. Adjust seasonings to taste.
Makes 4 cups.

Everyone will think you made this from scratch.

Rose Albertson
Arturo Toscanini Lodge #2107

TOMATO SAUCE

2 tablespoons olive oil
6 tablespoons butter
1½ cups chopped onions
1 tablespoon chopped garlic
¼ pound mushrooms, finely
    chopped
¾ cup finely chopped carrots
2 tablespoons finely chopped
    fresh parsley
1 tablespoon finely chopped
    fresh basil or 1 teaspoon
    dried basil

6 sprigs fresh thyme or 1
    teaspoon dried
1 teaspoon sugar
1 whole clove
½ cup dry white wine
4 cups chopped fresh or
    canned tomatoes
salt and freshly ground pepper
    to taste

Heat the oil and 2 tablespoons of butter in a heavy casserole. Add onions, garlic, mushrooms, carrots, parsley, basil, thyme, sugar and clove. Cook, stirring until the mixture is almost dry but still moist (about 10 minutes).

Add wine and continue stirring over high heat until wine evaporates. Add tomatoes, salt and pepper and bring to a boil. Partly cover and simmer one hour.

Put the mixture through a food mill, pushing through as much of the vegetable solids as possible. Stir in the remaining butter and bring to a boil.

Grace Messere
Utica Lodge #2054

MATALOCCO

1 (32 ounce) can crushed
tomatoes
8 cloves garlic, crushed

10 fresh basil leaves, cut up, or
1 teaspoon dry basil leaf
salt, pepper and some olive oil
a dash of oregano

Put all ingredients into bowl and marinate for 2 hours in refrigerator. When ready to serve, prepare a pound of linguine and serve over pasta.

Vita M. Conte
Edward J. Speno Lodge #2568

AGLIO E OLIO

(Garlic and Oil Sauce)

1 pound pasta
1 cup olive oil
4 cloves garlic, minced
⅓ cup minced, flat Italian
parsley
¼ teaspoon dried oregano

½ teaspoon salt
¼ teaspoon freshly ground
white pepper
freshly grated Parmesan or
Romano cheese for garnish

Heat oil until just fragrant. Add garlic and cook over a very low heat, stirring constantly, until garlic is barely golden. Stir in parsley, oregano, salt and pepper. Continue cooking and stirring for 1 minute. Serve over hot, drained spaghetti, linguini or other thin pasta. Top with grated cheese if desired.
Makes 4 to 6 servings.

Genevieve Lembo
Le Amiche Lodge #2550

VERMICELLI AGLIO E OLIO WITH ANCHOVIES

1 pound vermicelli or other
thin spaghetti
½ cup olive oil
1 tablespoon minced garlic
cloves

½ tablespoon parsley
(preferably fresh)
1 (2 ounce) can anchovies (flat
in oil)
½ teaspoon black pepper

Heat oil in a small skillet over low heat. Add garlic, stirring until the garlic turns golden. Add pepper, parsley and can of anchovies with oil, stir until anchovies dissolve. This takes about 5 minutes, and can be prepared the night before and refrigerated until needed.

Cook vermicelli or thin spaghetti as directed on package, preferably al dente. Drain vermicelli and immediately stir in the oil mixture. Serve hot.

Mary Spinelli Crescitelli
William C. LaMorte Lodge #2251

RED CLAM SAUCE

4 tablespoon olive oil
2 cloves garlic, chopped
1 onion, chopped
4 tomatoes, peeled, seeded and
chopped
2 tablespoons Italian parsley,
chopped

3-4 basil leaves, chopped
1 teaspoon oregano
3 dozen littleneck clams,
shucked with juice
1 pound linguine, cooked

Heat the oil in a saucepan. Add the garlic and onion. Cook until garlic is golden. Add tomatoes, parsley, basil and oregano and cook at least 8 to 10 minutes.

In small amount of water, add clams and bring to boil; simmer at least 5 minutes. Add clam juice to tomato sauce and simmer together 2 minutes. Pour over cooked pasta.
Serves 4 to 6.

Florence Bianca
Aquileia Ladies Lodge #935

WHITE WINE CLAM SAUCE

2 (6 ounce) cans whole clams
¼ cup thinly sliced green
   onion
1 clove garlic, minced
¼ cup olive oil
1 cup dry white wine

½ cup water
all of clam juice from drained
   clams
black pepper, cracked
Parmesan cheese, grated

Sauté onions and garlic in olive oil until tender. Stir in remaining liquid. Simmer gently, uncovered, about 8 to 10 minutes. Add clams, cook and stir for about 2 minutes until clams are heated through.

Serve with fresh cracked black pepper and freshly grated Parmesan cheese.

A chilled Meridian Chardonnay will compliment this dish.

Martha Marino
Giosue Carducci Lodge #226A

MARINARA SAUCE I

4-6 cloves garlic
1 small onion
½ cup oil
1 (32 ounce) can crushed
   tomatoes

1 teaspoon salt
pepper to taste
1 teaspoon oregano
1 teaspoon chopped fresh
   parsley or dried parsley

Sauté onion and garlic in oil until soft. Add tomatoes and spices. Simmer for about 30 minutes.

Carol Piccirillo
Gabriele D'Annunzio Lodge #321

MARINARA SAUCE II

1 large can peeled Italian style
   tomatoes or crushed
   tomatoes
2 cloves garlic
3 tablespoons olive oil

1 tablespoon Parmesan cheese
1 tablespoon chopped parsley
½ teaspoon sugar (optional)
salt and pepper to taste

Coarsely chop tomatoes in blender and set aside. If using crushed tomatoes, just open can and set aside.

Sauté garlic in olive oil, lightly in saucepan.

Add blended tomatoes, grated cheese, parsley, salt, pepper and sugar. Cook on a medium flame for about 15 minutes, stirring occasionally. *Yield: Serves 4 to 5 people.*

Michael A. Bologna
Mario Lanza Lodge #2491

GNOCCHI

6 medium-sized potatoes
3½ cups flour

1 small egg

Cook potatoes in salted water for about 20 minutes or until tender when pierced with fork.

Measure flour into bowl and add mashed, hot potatoes and egg. Mix well to make a soft elastic dough.

Turn dough onto a lightly floured surface and knead. Break off small pieces of dough and using the palm of your hand to roll pieces one-half inch in diameter. Cut into pieces about 1 inch long.

Curl each piece by pressing lightly with index finger and pulling the finger along the piece of dough toward you. Gnocchi may also be shaped by pressing each piece lightly with a floured fork.

Cook in boiling water to which 2 tablespoons salt has been added, for about 10 minutes.
Serves 4.

Gloria Ruggiero-Trofinoff
St. Francis of Assisi Lodge #2629

GNOCCHI DI SPINACI ALLA RICOTTA

(Spinach and Ricotta Dumplings)

1 (10 ounce) package frozen
  chopped spinach
¾ pound ricotta or cottage
  cheese
1 teaspoon salt
2 egg yolks

6 tablespoons grated Parmesan
  cheese
1 cup flour
hot water
¼ cup melted margarine or
  butter
1 teaspoon chopped parsley

Cook spinach and drain well. Combine spinach, ricotta cheese, salt, egg yolks and 3 tablespoons Parmesan cheese. Drop mixture from a spoon into flour and shape into balls. Cook in large amount of simmering water about 5 minutes. Remove; drain on towel. Pour margarine over dumplings; sprinkle with remaining grated Parmesan cheese and parsley.
Makes 6 servings.

Catherine A. Perry
Geneva American Italian Ladies Lodge #2397A

POLENTA WITH SAUSAGE

1 pound Italian sausage
1 small chopped onion
¼ teaspoon salt
1 medium can tomatoes
2 tablespoons water
1 clove sliced garlic

⅛ teaspoon pepper
2 small cans puree
1 pound cornmeal
1¼ quarts boiling salted water
  (2 tablespoons salt)
3 tablespoons grated cheese

Place sausage in large saucepan with 2 tablespoons water and pierce the sausage with a fork. Let it brown in its own juices. Add onion, garlic, salt and pepper and let brown a little longer. Add tomatoes and puree and simmer for 1½ hours. When sauce is cooked, pour cornmeal into boiling salted water. Stir constantly with wooden spoon for 30 minutes. Pour cornmeal onto large platter and pour tomato sauce over it. Place the cooked sausage around and sprinkle with the grated cheese.

Doris Collins
America Lodge #2245

POLENTA
(Microwave Style)

4 cups water
1¼ cups cornmeal
2 teaspoons salt, or to taste

dash of pepper
3 tablespoons butter

Combine water, cornmeal and salt in a 2½-quart dish. Cook uncovered at high power for 12 minutes, stirring once. Remove from oven. Stir in butter and a dash of pepper. Serve at once.
Makes about 4 servings.

Time given is for a 650 to 700 watt oven.

Dorothea Yarcel
Aida Ladies Lodge #2163A

BASIC POLENTA

9 cups water
1 tablespoon salt

3 cups coarse grain cornmeal

Bring water to a boil in large heavy pot. Add salt and reduce heat until water is simmering. Take cornmeal by the handful and add to water very slowly, controlling the flow to a thin stream through your fingers. To avoid lumps, stir quickly with a long-handled wooden spoon while adding cornmeal. If necessary stop adding cornmeal from time to time and beat mixture vigorously. Cook, stirring constantly, 20 to 30 minutes. Polenta will become very thick while cooking. It is done when it comes away cleanly from sides of pot. Pour polenta onto a large wooden board or a large platter. Wet your hands and smooth out polenta evenly about 2 inches thick. Let cook 5 to 10 minutes or until polenta solidifies. Cut cooled polenta into slices 1 inch wide and 6 inches long. Place slices in individual dishes. Serve hot with your favorite sauce.
Makes 6 to 8 servings.

Valerie Gobbo
Daughters of Columbus Lodge #1666

CANNELONI

1 large onion, chopped
2 large handfuls grated cheese
1 package chopped spinach
5 slices white bread
¼ pound margarine

1 pound lean ground beef
3 beaten eggs
½ pound soft cream cheese
manicotti shells, cooked
al dente

Sauté onion in margarine. Cook spinach 1 minute. Cook and squeeze spinach, add to onion and sauté 1 minute. Add beef and cook till pink disappears. Add eggs, salt and pepper. Blend in soft cream cheese. Add grated cheese and bread, crumbled. Mix together, fill shells. Ladle light marinara or Alfredo sauce over top and bake uncovered about 25 minutes.

Bea Corrao
Constantino Brumidi Ladies Auxiliary

RIGATONI WITH FOUR CHEESES

1 pound rigatoni
1½ cups half and half cream
3 ounces Gorgonzola cheese,
  crumbled
3 ounces Bel Paese cheese,
  cubed

3 ounces Fontina cheese, cubed
½ cup freshly grated cheese
2 tablespoons chopped parsley
salt and pepper

Cook pasta in large pot of boiling salted water. Simmer all cheeses in a large skillet on low heat. Drain pasta and add sauce. Season with salt and pepper to taste.

Connie Di Bella
Daughters and Sons of Italian Heritage Lodge #2428

PENNE WITH CAULIFLOWER

1½ pounds cauliflower, trimmed and broken into florets
¼ cup extra-virgin olive oil
2 large garlic cloves, minced
6 flat anchovy fillets, finely chopped
¼ teaspoon hot pepper flakes
1 pound penne
3 tablespoons grated Romano cheese
2 tablespoons chopped fresh parsley

Cook cauliflower in a large saucepan of boiling salted water until tender, 6 to 8 minutes. Drain in a colander, set aside.

In a large frying pan, heat olive oil over medium-low heat. Add garlic, anchovies, and hot pepper flakes. Cook, mashing with back of a spoon 1 to 2 minutes, or until anchovies dissolve. Add cauliflower to the pan, toss to coat with oil, and heat through, 1 to 2 minutes.

Meanwhile, cook penne in a large pot of boiling salted water until tender but still firm, 8 to 10 minutes, drain. Add penne to cauliflower and cook, tossing, for 1 minute. Remove from heat and toss in Romano cheese and parsley.
Serves 6.

Preparation time is 20 minutes.

This is a very basic recipe, useful for vegetable sauces. Broccoli and bitter greens are also good this way.

Grace Messere
Utica Lodge #2054

PENNE ALFRESCO

1 pound penne
½ cup olive oil
½ cup Parmesan cheese
8 fresh plum tomatoes
1 tablespoon fresh chopped parsley
1 tablespoon fresh chopped scallions
3 cloves garlic, chopped
½ cup fresh basil, chopped
salt and pepper to taste

Cook pasta al dente. Dice tomatoes and combine with all ingredients. Toss and pour over hot drained pasta adding cheese to taste. When cooking pasta, be sure to add salt to water.

Rose Cafaro
St. Thomas Aquinas Lodge #2569

PENNE WITH MUSHROOMS

1 pound fresh mushrooms
3 cloves garlic
½ cup fresh flat parsley
¼ cup olive oil

1 pound penne
grated Italian cheese
1-2 cans of chicken broth

Wipe mushrooms with damp cloth, cut into small pieces and set aside. Dice fresh parsley, set aside. Cut garlic into small pieces or put through garlic press. Heat olive oil over low flame, add garlic. Do not let it burn. Add parsley and cook for one minute. Add mushrooms, cover and cook for 2 minutes. Add chicken broth and black pepper to taste. Serve over penne with grated Italian cheese of your choice. *Serves 4 to 6.*

Veronica Martino
William C. LaMorte Lodge #2251

PENNE WITH BROCCOLI
AND SUN-DRIED TOMATOES

1 bunch broccoli
8 sun-dried tomatoes
1-2 cloves garlic
3-4 tablespoons olive (or more)

1 pound penne
chicken broth
Parmesan or Pecorino-Romano
  cheese

Parboil broccoli. Add sun-dried tomatoes sliced julienne-style, garlic, and olive oil. Sauté all of the above for a few minutes and then pour over 1 pound of cooked penne. Add ½ to 1 cup of pasta water or chicken broth to the pasta. Mix well and serve. Use Parmesan or Pecorino-Romano cheese.

Viola Tursi
Arturo Toscanini Lodge #2107

FETTUCCINE WITH SHRIMP AND PEAS

1 pound medium shrimp
  (cleaned)
1 egg
1 stick butter
1 pint heavy cream or half and
  half
1 medium onion, diced

1 small clove garlic, minced
1 (10 ounce) package frozen
  peas
1 pound fettuccine
Locatelli-Romano cheese,
  grated

Melt butter. Add onion and garlic. Sauté until onions are translucent. Add cream and heat making sure cream does not boil. Add defrosted peas to cream sauce. Add beaten egg to warm cream sauce, being careful not to cook egg. Remove from heat.

Microwave shrimp until pink in color and add to sauce. Add grated cheese to taste. Cook fettuccine according to directions. Drain and add sauce tossing until noodles are coated. Add additional grated cheese and freshly ground pepper. Serve immediately.
Yield: 4 servings.

Vicki Ann Cangemi Ahlsen
Donatello Lodge #2559

FETTUCCINE WITH ANCHOVY,
GARLIC AND LEMON

½ pound fettuccine
3 tablespoons olive oil
4 cloves garlic, minced
1 (2 ounce) can chopped
  anchovy fillets, drained

½ teaspoon grated lemon zest
¼ cup calamata olives, pitted
3 tablespoons chopped parsley
¼ cup lemon juice

Heat oil in frying pan. Add garlic, cook 30 to 60 seconds, do not brown. Add chopped anchovy fillets, stirring 1 minute longer. Stir in lemon juice and boil until blended and thickened, about 1 minute. Stir in olives, pepper to taste and parsley. Pour sauce over cooked fettuccine and sprinkle with lemon zest.

Jeanette Bonardi
Romanesque Lodge #2198

FETTUCCINE ALLA CARBONARA

8 strips bacon
6 ounces thickly sliced
    prosciutto
1½ sticks unsalted butter
2 tablespoons finely chopped
    onion
½ cup dry white wine
½ cup heavy cream

½ cup milk
1 tablespoon chopped fresh
    parsley
⅓ cup grated Parmesan cheese
1 egg yolk, lightly beaten
1 pound fresh-cut fettuccine
additional grated Parmesan
    cheese and black pepper

Bring 4 to 5 quarts salted water to full rolling boil in large pot. In a frying pan, cook bacon and drain it thoroughly. Cut prosciutto and bacon into ½-inch squares and set aside.

Melt butter in large saucepan, add onions and sauté over moderate to low heat until onion is translucent. Add bacon and prosciutto, and stir over low heat for 3 to 4 minutes. Stir in wine, increase heat, and bring mixture to a slow boil for 5 minutes while stirring.

Add cream and milk, and return to low boil again. Lower heat and add parsley and grated Parmesan cheese. Keep warm until pasta is ready.

When pasta water boils, add fettuccine all at once, and stir to separate strands. Return to a boil, and cook for 5 to 6 minutes or until done, stirring frequently. Drain well in a colander.

Pour hot bacon mixture over pasta, add egg yolk and toss until thoroughly combined. Serve immediately.

Gloria Colantone
Ann Bambino Lodge #2353

FETTUCCINE WITH SAUSAGE AND VEGETABLES

½ pound thin Italian sausage
   cut in 1-inch pieces
1 small yellow squash, diced
1 small zucchini, diced
½ cup chicken broth
¼ teaspoon white pepper

1 tablespoon garlic in oil
1½ red onions, diced
1 small tomato, peeled, seeded
   and diced
1 (9 ounce) package fresh
   fettuccine

Spray pan with Pam. Sauté sausage, tomato, garlic with onion, squash and zucchini for 5 minutes. Add sausage, pepper and broth. Cover and steam 5 minutes. Cook fettuccine as per package directions, drain and place in bowl. Mix sausage and vegetables. Sprinkle with Parmesan cheese.
Serves 2.

Loretta Howe
Anthony Casamento Lodge #2612

PASTIERRA

1 pound linguine
1 dozen eggs
lard, salt and pepper to taste

grated cheese (about 8
   tablespoons)

Coat large rectangular pan with lard. Cook and cool macaroni in its own water. Drain. Sprinkle 8 tablespoons grated cheese throughout macaroni. Mix in eggs, salt and pepper. Pour into large rectangular pan. Coat top of macaroni with dabs of lard. Cook at 350° in oven for ½ hour or until top is brown.

This is a good pasta dish that can also be cut up into little squares for hor d'oeuvres.

Grace Ferrara
Cellini Lodge #2206

LINGUINE CON GAMBERI E BROCCOLI

(Linguine with Shrimp and Broccoli)

20 extra-large shrimp
3 cloves garlic, finely chopped
1 cup warm water
2 chicken bouillon cubes
6 tablespoons white wine
2 tablespoons tomato sauce
   (for color)
1 tablespoon fresh parsley,
   chopped

2 ounces butter (½ stick)
1 large head broccoli (cut in
   large florets)
¾ pound linguine
2 tablespoons salt
garlic powder, paprika and
   oregano to taste

Preheat oven to 350°. Arrange shrimp in baking dish. Cut butter into thin slices and place over shrimp. Sprinkle fresh garlic, tomato sauce, parsley, wine, garlic powder, paprika and oregano over shrimp. Dissolve bouillon in water and pour over shrimp. Bake for 20 to 25 minutes. Set aside.

In a large pot of boiling salted water, blanch broccoli. Remove broccoli and add linguine. Cook linguine until done. Drain linguine and place on serving platter. Pour small amount of shrimp broth over linguine. Arrange 5 shrimp and 3 broccoli florets over the linguine in a circle. Pour remaining shrimp broth over linguine and serve immediately. *Makes 4 servings.*

Anthony J. Misso
Father John Papallo Kings Park Lodge #2684

LINGUINE WITH CAULIFLOWER

1 head of cauliflower (whole)
1 onion, sliced
olive oil

1 tablespoon pignoli nuts
1 tablespoon raisins
1 pound linguine or fusilli

Steam or boil head of cauliflower. Drain and refrigerate until cold (several hours). In large frying pan, sauté sliced onion in olive oil until golden. Put cauliflower in pan and mash with potato masher until brown. Add oil if necessary. Add 1 tablespoon pignoli nuts and 1 tablespoon raisins. Stir and serve over fusilli or linguine.

Veronica Martino
William C. LaMorte Lodge #2251

LINGUINE WITH SEAFOOD

2 pounds mussels
1 pound shrimp
1 dozen small clams
1 whole lobster
6 pieces chopped garlic
1 large onion, minced
¾ cup virgin olive oil
¼ cup butter

basil leaves
chopped parsley
2 bay leaves
½ cup dry white wine
oregano to taste
4 large cans plum tomatoes
hot pepper to taste

Clean and wash all of the seafood. Cut lobster into 8 pieces. Sauté the onion, garlic and parsley in a large pot with half of the oil and butter. Add the mussels and bay leaves. Sauté a few minutes. Then add ¼ cup of white wine and half of the crushed tomatoes. Simmer for 15 minutes.

Put the rest of the oil and butter in a large skillet with spices and herbs and cook for 5 minutes. On low flame, add shrimp, lobster, clams and white wine. Sauté 5 to 10 minutes and then add the rest of the tomatoes and hot pepper. Cool 5 minutes. Then add everything into the pot with the mussels and simmer for 10 to 15 minutes. Serve over cooked linguine.

Matteo Guiliano
Guiseppe Verdi Lodge #2163

PASTA....A LA MATAROCCO

1 pound linguine or
  Margherite

Sauce:

8-10 cloves garlic	black pepper
½ cup olive oil	salt
25-30 leaves of fresh basil	crushed red pepper
10-15 leaves of fresh mint	grated Italian cheese
2-3 overripe tomatoes	

Crush garlic and place into a bowl and add olive oil; chop fresh basil and fresh mint. Put all ingredients in a saucepan and cook for 1 minute. Peel tomatoes, crush and add to bowl and add black pepper, salt, and crushed red pepper.

Cook pasta al dente. Drain, saving a cup of pasta water. Add sauce in bowl on top of the hot pasta. Add a little water if needed. Serve with grated Italian cheese of your choice.

This is a traditional pasta dish that is indigenous to the province of Trapani, Sicily and especially so, it is most popular in the city of Marsala. The Marsalisi call it Pasta Matarocco.

Frank Bonetti
Mario Lanza Lodge #2491

SPAGHETTI ALLA RUSTICA

1 pound medium shrimp
½ cup extra-virgin olive oil
2 garlic cloves
crushed dried red chile pepper
   to taste

2 cups finely chopped, tender
   wild fennel tops
pinch dried oregano
salt
1 pound imported spaghetti
½ cup toasted bread crumbs

Clean and devein shrimp. In a large pan, sauté the extra-virgin olive oil, garlic and red chile pepper. Sauté for 2 to 3 minutes. Add shrimp, oregano and salt and sauté over high heat for about 4 minutes or until shrimp are just opaque. Meanwhile, cook the spaghetti and fennel tops in abundant boiling salted water until pasta is al dente. Quickly drain and toss with the shrimp and flavored oil. Sprinkle toasted bread crumbs, toss again and serve.

Joseph Colello
Rockland Lodge #2176

SPAGHETTI WITH CALAMARI

1 pound squid
¼ cup extra-virgin olive oil
1 onion, peeled and chopped
2 handfuls chopped Italian
   parsley
3 garlic cloves, peeled and
   chopped

1 cup dry red wine
1 (28 ounce) can imported
   Italian tomatoes
salt and pepper to taste
1 pound spaghetti

Clean fresh squid, cut into ¼-inch rings. Heat olive oil, add onion, parsley and garlic until lightly brown. Add cleaned and drained, cut-up squid; sauté briefly and add red wine. Add can of tomatoes and cook over low heat for 1½ hours or until the squid is completely tender.

Cook pasta al dente then add squid and tomato sauce.

John Buffa
Rockland Lodge #2176

PASTA A LA VODKA

1½ pounds pasta (rigatoni, penne, etc.)
salt to taste
7 tablespoons butter
½ teaspoon dried red pepper

1 cup Polish or Russian vodka
1 can whole Italian tomatoes with puree
1 cup heavy cream
½ cup grated cheese

Bring water to a boil. Add pasta.

Meanwhile melt butter in a saucepan large enough to hold the pasta when cooked. Add pepper and vodka. Bring to a boil, let it simmer 2 minutes. Add tomatoes and cream. Let it simmer. When pasta is cooked, drain.

Add pasta to the sauce. Mix thoroughly and serve immediately.

Edith Zuzolo
Arturo Toscanini Lodge #2107

PASTA PUTTANESCA

3 tablespoons olive oil
2 minced garlic cloves
2 ounces or more calamata black olives, pitted and chopped
1 teaspoon capers, coarsely chopped
1 large fresh tomato, peeled and coarsely chopped

4 or 5 anchovy fillets, coarsely chopped (optional)
1 pound spaghettini
⅓ cup finely chopped parsley
½ teaspoon salt
½ teaspoon pepper, freshly ground
1 teaspoon crushed red pepper flakes (optional)

Place the oil in a frying pan and add minced garlic. When it is golden, add the olives, capers, tomato and anchovy fillets. Stir well and heat through for about 6 minutes. Cook and drain pasta al dente. Place in a warm bowl and add half the sauce. Toss well. Add the remaining sauce on top. Sprinkle with parsley, salt and pepper to taste. Optional: Sprinkle red pepper flakes on top. Serve hot.

Angela Anselmo
Giovanni Caboto Lodge #2372

FRITTATA DI PASTA

6 extra-large eggs
¼ teaspoon salt
freshly milled pepper to taste
5 tablespoons Parmigiano-Reggiano cheese
3 tablespoons fresh basil or parsley leaves, chopped coarsely

2 sweet Italian sausage links, boiled and sliced, or crumbled
2 cups (½ pound) leftover pasta with tomato sauce
2 tablespoons olive oil

Lightly beat the eggs with the salt, pepper, Parmigiano and basil or parsley. Mix well with the sausage and the cooked, sauced pasta. Heat the oil in a 12-inch frying pan or omelet pan. When it is hot enough to make the eggs sizzle, add the mixture to the pan using a fork or spoon to distribute the sausage and pasta evenly.

Cook over very gentle heat 12 to 15 minutes until the frittata is set, but not browned. Because of the density of this frittata, it will be necessary to rotate the pan on the burner throughout the cooking time so that all parts of the frittata are cooked evenly.

To finish off the top, slide the pan 6 inches under the broiler for 1 minute or less, until the surface is golden.

Serve warm or cold, cut into wedges.
Makes 5 servings.

Rosalie Galatioto
Giovanni Caboto Lodge #2372

PASTA WITH PINE NUTS AND SUN-DRIED TOMATOES

12 ounces fusilli or other spiral
    pasta
5 tablespoons olive oil
⅔ cup pine nuts

⅔ cup chopped, drained, oil-
    packed, sun-dried tomatoes
½ cup chopped fresh parsley
½ cup grated Parmesan cheese

Cook fusilli pasta al dente. Drain well. Heat 3 tablespoons olive oil in large skillet over high heat. Add pasta and fry until beginning to crisp at edges, stirring frequently, about 10 minutes. Transfer pasta to large bowl. Add remaining 2 tablespoons olive oil to same skillet. Add toasted pine nuts and sun-dried tomatoes and stir over high heat until just warmed through, about 1 minute. Pour the mixture over the pasta. Add chopped parsley and Parmesan cheese; toss to blend. Season to taste with salt and pepper.

Ana Zingarello
Raffaello Lodge #2661

PASTA WITH BREAD CRUMBS

½ cup olive oil
1½ cups bread crumbs
4 cloves garlic, chopped
fresh parsley, chopped

salt to taste
pepper to taste
1 pound spaghetti

In large skillet, sauté chopped garlic in olive oil until golden brown. When garlic is sautéed, add bread crumbs, blend together and cook on low flame until deep brown and nicely moistened. Prepare spaghetti, drain and pour bread crumb mixture over top of pasta and fold together.

Sprinkle grated cheese to taste and serve hot.

Carol DiTrapani
Per Sempre Ladies Lodge #2344A

SEAFOOD PASTA

¼ cup olive oil
2 cloves garlic, chopped
1 tablespoon oregano, or to
taste
salt and pepper to taste
1 large (28 ounce) can crushed
tomatoes
½ cup white wine

dash of hot pepper flakes,
optional
½ pound uncooked shrimp,
peeled and deveined
½ pound scallops
1 pound uncooked spaghetti
2 tablespoons fresh chopped
parsley

In large skillet, heat olive oil and sauté garlic. Stir in oregano, salt and pepper. Add tomatoes, pepper flakes and wine; simmer for about 15 minutes. Add shrimp and scallops and cook until done, about 5 minutes.

Cook spaghetti according to package directions, al dente. Drain and place on serving platter. Pour seafood sauce over pasta and sprinkle with parsley.
Makes 4 servings.

All shrimp or all scallops may be substituted. Using fresh spinach angel hair pasta makes a colorful, delicious repast.

Bill Howe
Anthony Casamento Lodge #2612

PASTA WITH PEAS

1 large onion, sliced thin
2 tablespoons olive oil
7 cups water
1 (16 ounce) can peas

½ pound ditali
salt and pepper to taste
grated cheese

Sauté onion in oil until lightly browned. Add 7 cups water and peas. Simmer 30 minutes. Add ½ pound ditali pasta and salt and pepper to taste. When cooked, serve with grated cheese sprinkled on top.
Serves 4 as a first dish.

Mary DiScala
Cellini Lodge #2206

PASTA WITH BROCCOLI RABE AND SAUSAGE

3 pounds broccoli rabe
1½ pounds Italian sausage
2 cloves garlic (whole or
    minced)
dash of hot pepper

salt according to taste
1 tablespoon olive oil
1 cup fresh tomato sauce
1 pound orrechetti pasta

Remove tough stems from broccoli, wash and leave in water until ready for them.

Heat oil in large pot. Cut sausage into bite-size pieces, or if preferred, remove from casing and sauté until brown. Add garlic, tomato sauce and seasoning.

Remove broccoli from water and chop up into bite-size pieces. Add to the sausage. Cover and cook for about 10 minutes or until the broccoli is cooked. Serve over orrechetti pasta topped with Pecorino Romano cheese.
Serves 4.

Laura LoCurto Cheresnik
Italian Heritage Lodge #2227

PASTA CARBONARA

(Coal Miners' High Protein Dinner)

1 pound spaghetti or linguini
3 strips bacon
½ pound butter
1 cup Romano cheese
1 small onion

2 cloves garlic
salt and pepper to taste
3 tablespoons oil (olive or
   vegetable)
2 large or 3 small eggs

Cook pasta a trifle more than al dente.

Sauté garlic, butter, bacon, salt, pepper and finely chopped onion until onion is transparent. Just before adding to pasta, mix in half the cheese.

Thoroughly beat the eggs. Place the cooked pasta in a pot with a tight-fitting cover. Cover the pasta with the sauce and the eggs and mix thoroughly. When mixed, cover the pot. Let stand for a couple of minutes. The heat from the cooked pasta will cook the eggs.

Just before serving, sprinkle the rest of the cheese over the pasta.

Joe Colello
Rockland Lodge #2176

CHICKEN PASTA

4 ounces uncooked mostaccioli
  (about 1½ cups)
2 cups sliced fresh mushrooms
1 cup broccoli florets
1 cup thinly sliced carrots
1 cup milk
1 tablespoon cornstarch

2 teaspoons chopped fresh
  parsley
¼ teaspoon salt
1 clove garlic, finely chopped
2 cups shredded spinach
1½ cups cut-up cooked chicken
½ cup shredded Swiss cheese

Cook mostaccioli in 3-quart saucepan as directed on package, except add mushrooms, broccoli and carrots during the last 5 minutes of cooking.

Meanwhile, mix milk, cornstarch, parsley, salt and garlic in 1½-quart saucepan. Cook over medium heat until mixture thickens and boils. Stir in remaining ingredients until cheese is melted and spinach is wilted. Drain pasta mixture, toss with sauce.
Makes 4 servings.

Elvira Castellano
Anthony Casamento Lodge #2612

MANICOTTI

Shells:

2 cups flour   salt
2 eggs   butter
2 cups milk

Mix all ingredients together except butter. Grease small frying pan with butter. When butter is melted and pan is hot, put enough mix in bottom of pan just to cover. When it starts to bubble, turn to other side. When cooked, cool on wax paper and repeat process until all shells are made. Do not brown. Shells will cook very fast and consistency should be thin.

Stuffing:

2 pounds ricotta cheese   parsley to taste
1 large mozzarella cheese   grating cheese (optional)
1 egg

Slice mozzarella in small pieces and mix with stuffing ingredients. Add salt to taste. Grating cheese can also be added. Place stuffing in center of shell and flap both sides over. Place in pan; top with sauce. Bake approximately 20 to 30 minutes in a 350° oven.

Maryann Perticone
Constantino Brumidi Ladies Auxiliary

LASAGNA ROLL UPS

12-20 curly lasagna noodles,
   cooked and drained
12-20 slices of ham

2-3 packages broccoli spears,
   cooked and drained

Cheese Sauce:
¼ cup lowfat mayonnaise
4 tablespoons flour
½ teaspoon salt

dash of pepper
2 cups milk
2 cups mozzarella cheese

Make cheese sauce in small pot, stir together first 4 ingredients, stir constantly over medium heat. Gradually add milk and cheese until smooth, keep stirring until thickens.

Spoon ½ cheese sauce into 2-quart oblong baking dish. Place 1 slice ham and ½ broccoli on each lasagna. Roll up noodle, jelly-roll style. Place in baking pan and repeat until all noodles are used. Spoon remaining sauce over roll-ups and cover with foil. Bake at 350° for a half hour. Uncover and let stand for 15 minutes before serving.
Serves 12 to 20.

Millie Alessi
Dr. Vincenzo Sellaro Lodge #2319

VEGETARIAN LASAGNA

Filling:

1 cup spinach, chopped
(if using frozen spinach,
sauté it quickly in a little
butter and drain)

3 pounds ricotta cheese

2 cups grated mozzarella
cheese

1 cup of any grated soft mild
cheese (Cheddar, Monterey
Jack, or grated Parmesan)

salt and pepper to taste

Sauce:

½ cup olive oil

2 onions, peeled and finely
chopped

3 garlic cloves

1 carrot, grated

5 or 6 Porcini mushrooms,
cleaned and sliced

3 sun-dried tomatoes

1 teaspoon fresh parsley,
chopped

2 cups imported plum
tomatoes

salt and pepper to taste

In a large saucepan, heat olive oil and brown onions, garlic and mushrooms. Add remaining ingredients and cook for 1 hour over low heat, stirring constantly. Cool slightly and blend for 30 seconds in blender or food processor.

To Assemble: Have 1 box lasagna noodles and grated Parmesan cheese handy. Preheat oven to 350°. Prepare noodles according to package directions; drain. In a large flat pan, arrange a layer of noodles, then add a layer of filling and a layer of sauce; sprinkle with Parmesan cheese. Repeat all layers until pan is filled. Top with Parmesan cheese and bake for 1 hour.

Chris Parillo
Gabriele D'Annunzio Lodge #321

MEATLESS LASAGNA

1 onion
½ cup celery
6 ounces tomato paste
2 cloves garlic
½ cup carrots
½ cup sunflower seeds
¼ cup peanuts

2 tablespoons pine nuts
¾ cup water
½ cup red wine
8 ounces mozzarella cheese, shredded, and Parmesan cheese to taste

8 ounces finely chopped mushrooms
1 tablespoon oregano

1 (1 pound) can Roma plum tomatoes
2 tablespoons basil

Mince onion, celery, tomato paste, garlic, and carrots. Grind sunflower seeds, peanuts, and pine nuts. Add all remaining ingredients (except mozzarella and Parmesan cheeses) and simmer. Cook one pound of lasagna al dente. Layer lasagna with sauce only; top with mozzarella and grated cheese. Cover with foil and bake ½ hour. Before serving, leave 2 minutes uncovered.
Serves 4.

Laura LoCurto Cheresnik
Italian Heritage Lodge #2227

RAVIOLI AND TORTELLINI

1 (28 ounce) can tomato puree
1 (6 ounce) can tomato paste
1 medium onion
3 whole cloves garlic
6 pieces celery (1-inch size)
1 tablespoon parsley

5 or 6 leaves of fresh basil
½ teaspoon black pepper
10 sliced black pitted olives
2 tablespoons Parmesan cheese
½ pound ravioli
½ pound tortellini

Put all above ingredients, except for ravioli and tortellini, in a pot and simmer approximately 1½ hours.

Cook ½ pound ravioli and ½ pound tortellini in separate pots according to package directions.

Put pasta in bowl, pour sauce over pasta. Blend well. Top with Parmesan cheese.
Serves 5 to 6.

Lucy Cutrone
Per Sempre Ladies Lodge #2344A

NITA'S SPINACH LASAGNA

Have prepared:
tomato sauce

12 lasagna noodles (½ cooked, drained and rinsed in cold water)

Filling:
2 cups ricotta or cottage cheese
2 beaten eggs
½ pound raw spinach
1 pound shredded mozzarella cheese

½ cup grated Parmesan or Romano cheese
salt and pepper to taste

Spread enough sauce to cover bottom of pan. Cover with a layer of noodles. Spread filling mix evenly over noodles. Spread sauce evenly and continue with another layer of noodles, filling and sauce. Continue layering until all ingredients are used, ending with a final layer of sauce and Parmesan or Romano cheese. Bake 45 minutes at 375°. Let stand for 10 minutes before serving.

Enjoy!!

Representative Nita Lowey
U.S. House of Representatives

TORTELLINI PRIMAVERA IN ASPARAGUS SAUCE

1 pound tricolor cheese tortellini
2 pounds asparagus
1 stick of butter
1 small onion, chopped

salt to taste
heavy cream to taste
grated Parmesan cheese
parsley flakes

Wash and trim asparagus. Boil tips about 15 minutes. Heat butter in a skillet and add chopped onion. Sauté for about 3 minutes until golden brown. In separate pot of boiling water, add salt and cook the tricolor cheese tortellini for about 7 minutes. Drain well. Transfer tortellini to skillet and add heavy cream to taste. Stir gently till well blended. Add a generous amount of Parmesan cheese and parsley flakes.

Mario Cermele
Antonio Meucci Lodge #213

PASTA CON RICOTTA

(Macaroni and Cheese)

1 pound cut macaroni (any type)	½ cup milk
	2 ounces butter
1 pound ricotta cheese	½ cup Parmesan cheese

Cook macaroni until tender in 5 quarts rapidly boiling salted water. Drain, return macaroni to pot and add butter. Mix ricotta with milk in a bowl until smooth. Pour over hot macaroni.

Sprinkle with grated Parmesan cheese and serve hot.
Serves 4 to 6.

Josephine Baldanza
Romanesque Lodge #2198

ZUCCHINI RICE CASSEROLE

¼ zucchini, sliced and unpeeled	1 (8 ounce) package shredded Cheddar cheese
grated Romano cheese, to taste	1 can cream of mushroom soup
black pepper	1 can of water
1 cup of rice, raw	bread crumbs
	1 pound bacon

Spray a 9 x 13-inch pan with Pam and layer in order given.

Layer zucchini, sprinkle generously with grated Romano cheese and black pepper. Sprinkle raw rice. Sprinkle with shredded Cheddar cheese. Repeat above three ingredients for three layers. Dilute 1 can cream of mushroom soup and 1 can of water and mix well. Pour over ingredients. Sprinkle generously with bread crumbs. Cut 1 pound bacon strips in quarters and place on top of bread crumbs. Cover with aluminum foil and bake 2 hours at 300°. Uncover and continue baking another ½ hour at 400° or until bacon is done.

Toni Salamida Murphy
Daughters of Columbus Lodge #1666

BAKED RICE ITALIANO

¾ cup chopped onion
½ pound Italian sausage
1 tablespoon butter, margarine
  or canola oil
1 cup fresh or frozen peas

1 (2 ounce) can sliced
  mushrooms, drained
1 (8 ounce) can tomato sauce
3 cups cooked rice (see note)
½ cup grated Parmesan cheese

Preheat oven to 375°. Brown onion and sausage lightly in the melted butter. Add peas and mushrooms and stir. Cook for several minutes. Add tomato sauce, cover and simmer for 10 minutes. Combine with cooked rice and place in buttered 1-quart casserole. Bake for 15 to 20 minutes.
Serves 4.

Note: It's important to use Uncle Ben's converted rice; otherwise, the kernels may clump and stick together. Don't overcook the rice.

Marilyn DiBiase
Aida Ladies Lodge #2163A

EASY RICE PRIMAVERA

2 cups water
1 cup long grain rice
1 cup broccoli florets
½ cup chopped green peppers
½ cup diced tomatoes
1½ tablespoons Parmesan
  cheese

2½ cups Chablis or other dry
  wine
vegetable cooking spray
1 cup diced zucchini
2 cloves garlic, minced
2 tablespoons chopped parsley
freshly ground pepper

Bring water and wine to a boil, add rice, cover, reduce heat and simmer 20 minutes or until rice is tender and liquid is absorbed. Coat a nonstick skillet with cooking spray; place over medium heat until hot. Add broccoli and next three ingredients. Sauté 5 minutes or until crisp tender. Add broccoli mixture, tomatoes and parsley to rice, stirring well. Transfer to serving bowl, sprinkle with cheese and pepper.

Mary Scarapicchia
Daughters of Columbus Lodge #1666

RISOTTO WITH SAFFRON

7 cups fresh or canned chicken
   stock
1 cup dry white wine
good pinch saffron threads
2 tablespoons olive oil

2 cloves garlic, crushed
1 medium onion, diced
2 cups arborio rice (see note)
salt and pepper to taste
1 tablespoon chopped parsley

Bring the chicken stock, wine and saffron to a gentle simmer in a 4-quart pot. Heat another 4- to 6-quart pot and add the oil, garlic and onion. Sauté for 3 minutes and add the arborio rice. Sauté over low heat for 5 to 7 minutes to lightly toast the rice. Add 1 cup of the simmering stock to the toasted rice and cook over medium-low heat, stirring all the time until the rice absorbs the liquid.

Begin adding the remaining simmering stock ½ cup at a time, allowing the rice to absorb the liquid each time. Cook for about 30 minutes until all the stock has been used. Add salt and pepper to taste, and stir in the parsley.
Serves 6 to 8.

Note: Arborio is the most common form of superfino rice exported to the United States from Italy. While arborio costs a bit more than American rice, don't even think of substituting American for the arborio in risotto.

Chris Parillo
Gabriele D'Annunzio Lodge #321

RICE ARANCINI
(Rice Balls)

1 cup Carolina rice (uncooked)
4 tablespoons butter or
  margarine
2 teaspoons salt
¼ pound chop meat, raw
¼ cup frozen peas
1 small onion, chopped

1 (8 ounce) can tomato sauce
4 eggs
1 cup bread crumbs
¼ cup Parmesan cheese
½ teaspoon oregano
½ cup water

Cook rice according to package directions with 4 tablespoons butter and 1 teaspoon salt. Mix Parmesan cheese when rice is cooked and refrigerate. When rice is completely cooled, add 3 egg yolks. Mix well and refrigerate for 20 minutes.

Sauté onion. Add chop meat and brown for 2 minutes. Add 1 teaspoon salt, oregano, tomato sauce and water and cook for 15 minutes. Add frozen peas and cook for 5 minutes. Let cool completely and put in a strainer. Save the juices. Mix just enough juice with rice to give it a pink color. (Mix well).

To make rice balls, place some rice in the palm of your hand, forming a pocket. Put some of the chop meat mixture in the pocket and add enough rice to cover the pocket. Press together to form a ball. For best cooking results, refrigerate rice balls for 30 minutes before frying.

Meanwhile, beat 2 egg whites with 1 whole egg. Roll the rice balls in eggs, enough to coat. If they don't stay together well, refrigerate again. Roll the rice balls in bread crumbs, coat evenly and deep fry in hot oil until golden brown.
Makes 8 rice balls.

Anne and Rose Marano
Marco Polo Lodge #2214

ARANCINI DI SICILIANI

(Sicilian Rice Balls)

2 cups of Carolina rice,
   or 1 pound box
1 teaspoon salt
3 egg yolks (save whites)
¼ cup Romano cheese, grated
2 tablespoons butter
1 tablespoon finely minced
   fresh parsley

white or black pepper to taste
dash of garlic powder
4 cups bread crumbs
peanut oil for frying
1 tablespoon milk
mozzarella cheese

In a saucepan, bring 4 cups of water to a boil. Add rice, salt and butter and cook 15 to 20 minutes until all water is absorbed. Put rice into a large bowl and add egg yolks, cheese, parsley, pepper and garlic powder. Mix well with fork. Set aside for ½ hour or more and then shape into a ball (size of small orange). Poke a hole into center and insert a ½-inch cube of mozzarella cheese. Cover hole with rice and then roll in beaten egg whites that have been mixed with milk. Roll in bread crumbs and coat evenly. Set aside on platter for half hour. In a deep heavy pan, heat the peanut oil. Fry the balls until they are golden brown on all sides. Drain on brown paper or paper towel and serve immediately.

In addition to mozzarella cubes for filling, the following may be added or substituted; prosciutto, ham, tomato sauce, chopped beef, or peas.

Elena Quattrone
Giovanni Caboto Lodge #2372

CARNE, PESCE, POLLO

MEAT, FISH, CHICKEN

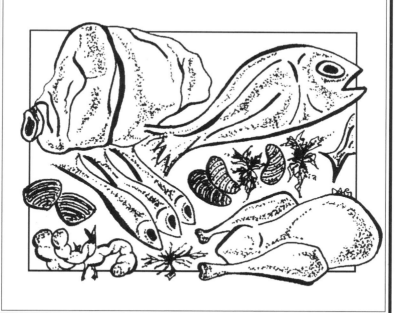

NEW YORK OSIA FILIAL LODGES

•**Cellini Lodge #2206**, New Hyde Park, Charter issued 1968: Benvenuto Cellini was an Italian Sculptor born in Florence in 1500. As a metalworker, he enjoyed the patronage of Pope Clement VII and later of Francis I of France. He is best known for the famous bronze statue "Perseus with the Head of Medusa". This is the home lodge of the current New York State President and President of the New York OSIA Grand Lodge Foundation, Joseph Sciame.

•**Filippo Mazzei Lodge #2207**, New City, Charter issued 1968: Philip Mazzei was one of America's founding Fathers and a confidant of President Thomas Jefferson. He was greatly esteemed in the United States. Mazzei was a political activist and writer during the War of Independence and has been credited with the conception of the famous phrase from the Declaration of Independence, "that all men are created equal".

•**Constantino Brumidi Lodge #2211**, Deer Park, Charter issued 1969: Constantino Brumidi, the "Michelangelo of the United States Capitol", decorated every important area of the Capitol including the great rotunda containing a frescoed frieze of fifteen historical groupings. His work was so admired that he was retained for the remainder of his life.

•**Vincent Linguanti Lodge #2212**, Monsey, Charter issued 1969: The name of Vincent Linguanti was taken to honor the memory of the first Italian-American who died in World War II from Rockland County.

•**Marco Polo Lodge #2214**, Levittown, Charter issued 1969: Marco Polo was an early Renaissance merchant and explorer who reached China overland in 1275.

•**Rocky Marciano Lodge #2226**, Oceanside, Charter issued 1970: Rocco Frances Marchegiano (Rocky Marciano) was an Italian-American boxer who won the heavy-weight championship in 1952 by knocking out the famous Joe Walcott. He retired as the only undefeated heavyweight champion in 1956.

•**Italian Heritage Lodge #2227**, New Rochelle, Charter issued 1970: Proud of its inheritance and traditions brought from Italy, this lodge was formed to preserve the Italian culture and language in the New Rochelle area.

•**Guglielmo Marconi Lodge #2232**, Islip, Charter issued 1970: Guglielmo Marconi was truly a pioneer of radio waves. He developed the "wireless telegraph" and went on to win the Nobel Prize in Physics in 1909.

•**Giuseppe A. Nigro Lodge #2234**, Brentwood, Charter issued 1970: Giuseppe Nigro of Glen Cove, a Past National Treasurer, was considered the godparent of many lodges on Long Island during the 1960's and 1970's. He was a self-made millionaire who maintained his humble beginnings throughout his entire life.

•**Etruscan Lodge #2238**, New Paltz, Charter issued 1971: The Etruscan civilization was considered the highest civilization in Italy before the rise of Rome. Their wealth was based partly on their knowledge of metalworking.

•**P. Vincent Landi Lodge #2239**, Rocky Point, Charter issued 1971: P. Vincent Landi served as New York OSIA State President from 1969 to 1973. He was a founder and first president of the Columbus Lodge #2143 and served as National Treasurer.

•**Jane H. Landi Lodge #2239A**, Shoreham, Charter issued 1976: Jane Landi was a devoted school teacher, parent and wife of P. Vincent Landi.

(Continued on next divider page)

SAUSAGE, PEPPER AND ONION SKILLET

1 pound sweet or hot fresh
   Italian sausage, cut into
   1-inch pieces
1 small onion or half a large
   onion, thinly sliced
   crosswise and separated
   into rings
1 large bell pepper, cored,
   seeded and cut into thin
   strips

2 large cloves garlic, finely
   chopped
½ cup dry vermouth or dry
   white wine
finely chopped parsley or
   other fresh or dry herbs
   (optional)

In a large skillet or sauté pan, brown sausage until it's cooked through. Remove from pan. Set aside.

Pour all but one tablespoon fat from pan. Add onions to pan. Cook over medium-high heat for 1 or 2 minutes. Add pepper and garlic. Cook 1 or 2 minutes more.

Return sausage to pan. Add vermouth or wine. Cook over high heat stirring constantly, until wine is reduced by about half. Remove from heat. Quickly stir in parsley or other herbs, if used. Serve immediately. *Serves 4.*

Preparation time: 20 minutes.

Adeline Moracco
Geneva American Italian Ladies Lodge #2397A

GLAZED PORK ROAST

2 teaspoons cornstarch
3 tablespoons Grand Marnier
8 ounces canned whole
   cranberry sauce

⅛ teaspoon each: pepper, salt,
   garlic and cinnamon
2 pounds trimmed, boneless
   pork loin

Place cornstarch, Grand Marnier, cranberry sauce and pepper, salt, garlic and cinnamon in a medium-size saucepan. Cook over medium heat until all mixture thickens. Set aside. Place roast in a 350° oven for 45 minutes. Spoon cranberry glaze over the roast. Continue cooking 45 minutes longer, basting every 10 minutes.
Serves 6.

Jean Oropallo
Constantino Brumidi Ladies Auxiliary

ROAST PORK WITH VEGETABLES

4 tablespoons olive oil
1 tablespoon lemon juice
1 clove garlic, minced
¼ teaspoon pepper
3½ pounds pork loin roast
    (ribs cracked)

¼ teaspoon savory, crushed
¼ teaspoon thyme, crushed
1 teaspoon salt
4 large baking potatoes

Preheat oven to 350°. In a small bowl, combine 2 tablespoons oil, lemon juice, garlic, salt, pepper, savory and thyme. With a fork, pierce roast all over. Rub in the oil mixture. Place in a large roasting pan. Bake 45 minutes. Meanwhile, cook potatoes in boiling water for 20 minutes. Drain, cut into quarters lengthwise. Brush with remaining oil. Place potatoes around roast turning to coat with juices. Bake ½ hour longer or until meat thermometer reads 170° and potatoes are fork-tender.

Maria Cicciarella
Constantino Brumidi Ladies Auxiliary

TRIPE WITH POTATOES

3 pounds tripe
1 onion, chopped
4 tablespoons olive oil
salt and pepper
½ teaspoon oregano
3 tablespoons tomato puree
1 tablespoon parsley

1 teaspoon basil
1 large can crushed tomatoes
4 large potatoes (cut into large
    cubes)
water as needed
hot pepper flakes (optional)

Wash tripe; remove all visible fat and cut into ½-inch strips. In 6-quart pot, cover tripe in plenty of water. On low heat, cook about 2 hours until tender with cover on. Remove from heat; let stand until water cools with cover on.

In saucepan, add oil, 1 large chopped onion and brown. Add 3 tablespoons of tomato puree and stir until golden. Add salt, pepper, parsley, oregano, basil and crushed tomatoes. Clean and cut 4 large potatoes, let cook ½ hour. Add tripe and cook ½ hour more. Hot pepper flakes are optional.

Joseph and Teresa Nacci
William Paca Lodge #2189

FEGATO ALLA VENEZIANA

(Calf's Liver, Venice Style)

1 pound calf's liver	3 tablespoons chopped fresh
1 (4 ounce) onion	Italian parsley
1 tablespoon unsalted butter	salt and pepper to taste
1 tablespoon olive oil	

Remove membranes from liver and cut into very thin slices. Peel and slice the onion. Melt butter with oil in a skillet and sauté onion for 2 minutes. Add liver slices and sauté for 5 minutes, browning on both sides.

Sprinkle with parsley and season to taste and serve without delay.

Mary Castaldo
Aquileia Ladies Lodge #935

PORCUPINES

(Meatballs)

1 pound ground beef	½ teaspoon salt and a little
½ cup uncooked rice	black pepper
1 large clove garlic, minced	1 jar Ragu spaghetti sauce,
½ medium onion, minced	any flavor

Mix beef, rice and seasonings and shape into small balls. Place in deep baking dish. Mix sauce with ¾ cup water and pour over rice and meatballs. Sprinkle top with oregano and bake 1½ to 2 hours at 325°.

When cooked, rice will protrude from meatballs resembling porcupines.

Rose De Yulio
Geneva Italian American Ladies Lodge #2397A

ITALIAN MEATBALLS

1 pound ground beef
1 teaspoon garlic powder
2 eggs
4-5 slices bread, soaked in
    water and squeezed dry

¼ cup grated cheese
1½ teaspoons salt
¼ teaspoon pepper
handful of parsley flakes

Mix all ingredients together. Shape into round balls and fry in hot oil until evenly browned.

JoAnn Testani
Stella D'Argento Lodge #1916

MEATLOAF

(Pizzaiola Style)

1 pound ground beef
¼ cup Parmesan cheese
1 egg
3 slices white bread (crust
    removed), pre-soaked in
    milk
1 clove garlic, chopped fine

1 (8-ounce) wedge mozzarella
    cheese, diced
salt and pepper to taste
4 potatoes, peeled and cut into
    wedges
2 onions, sliced fine
marinara sauce

Mix ground beef with salt, pepper, garlic, cheese, bread and egg; blend thoroughly. Add ½ cup marinara sauce and mix well.

Shape into an oblong loaf and place in large deep roasting pan that has been greased lightly with oil. Make a long well down the center of meatloaf. Put diced mozzarella cheese in well and seal, covering mozzarella cheese with meat. Arrange potatoes and onions around meatloaf. Pour marinara sauce over meatloaf, potatoes and onions.

Cover and bake in 350° oven until potatoes are tender (approximately 1½ hours).
Yield: Serves 4 to 5 people.

Michael A. Bologna
Mario Lanza Lodge #2491

SICILIAN MEAT ROLL

2 pounds ground beef
¾ cup bread crumbs
2 eggs (beaten)
½ cup tomato juice
2 tablespoons chopped parsley
1 clove garlic (crushed)

½ teaspoon oregano
¼ teaspoon salt
¼ teaspoon pepper
½ pound prosciutto
½ pound mozzarella cheese

Combine beef, bread crumbs, eggs, tomato juice, parsley, garlic, oregano, salt and pepper. Mix well. Place beef on waxed paper and shape into rectangle. Place prosciutto on beef, leaving an inch at edges. Cut 3 slices mozzarella and put aside. Grate remaining cheese over prosciutto.

Roll like a jelly roll and place seam side down in roasting pan. Bake for 45 minutes at 350°.

Cut cheese slices in half diagonally and place on top of roll. Return to oven and bake 5 minutes more.

Harriet Sturiano
Per Sempre Ladies Lodge #2344A

SICILIAN BREADED STEAK

4 boneless club or rib steaks,
    ¼- to ½-inch thick
1 cup bread crumbs
1 teaspoon oregano

salt and pepper to taste
¼ cup chopped onions
⅓ cup olive oil

Mix bread crumbs, onions, salt and pepper. Spread olive oil over steaks (use fingers). Dip oiled steaks into bread mixture (both sides). Place in broiling pan. Broil until bread crumbs "toast" or as desired. *Serves 4.*

Florence Gatto
Giovanni Caboto Lodge #2372

STEAK PIZZIOLA I

2 (14 ounce) sirloin steaks
1 tablespoon butter
½ tablespoon oregano
8 ounces fresh mushrooms

8 ounces tomato sauce
2 tablespoons heavy cream
½ ounce prosciutto
salt and pepper to taste

Broil steaks to preference in frying pan. Sauté butter with mushrooms, oregano and prosciutto. Add tomato sauce and heavy cream. Cook 8 to 12 minutes.

Serve with side dish of pasta or with accompanying vegetables.

Buon Appetito!

Rose Albertson
Arturo Toscanini Lodge #2107

STEAK PIZZAIOLA II

1 large chuck steak
salt and pepper

basil leaf
oregano

Sauce:
⅓ cup olive oil
3 cloves garlic
1 teaspoon salt
½ teaspoon ground black
    pepper

4 cups fresh tomatoes, peeled
    and chopped
2 tablespoons parsley

Heat olive oil in heavy saucepan and add garlic. Cook over medium heat for 2 minutes. Add tomatoes and remaining ingredients and cook over medium heat for 15 to 20 minutes.

Brown steak and cover with sauce. Bake in oven for 45 minutes to 1 hour.

Serve with rice or spaghetti.

Genevieve Lembo
Le Amiche Lodge #2550

BRISKET

4-6 pounds of brisket, trim fat
1 (12 ounce) can of beer
1 package onion soup mix

1 cup ketchup
1 can whole berry cranberry
  sauce

Season meat with garlic powder. Combine remaining ingredients and pour over meat. Cook covered 2½ to 3 hours at 350°.

This should be cooked at least one day in advance so the meat can marinate. It can be prepared far in advance and frozen. Slice before freezing.

Warm and serve.

Honorable Claire I. Weinberg
Judge, District Court of Nassau County

LAMB SHANKS AND WHITE BEANS

4 lamb shanks
¼ cup flour
¼ cup olive oil
3 medium onions, sliced
3 large cloves garlic, minced
1 teaspoon rosemary
dash of salt
2 teaspoons black pepper

1 (1 pound, 1 ounce) can Italian
  peeled tomatoes
2 tablespoons seasoned bread
  crumbs
2 tablespoons grated Parmesan
  cheese
2 (1 pound, 4 ounce) cans
  cannellini beans

Rub lamb shanks with flour. Brown meat on all sides in oil in heavy pan. Remove when browned. Sauté onion and garlic in same pan about 5 minutes. Add rosemary, salt, pepper and tomatoes with their liquid, to onion and garlic.

Add lamb, cover, cook slowly for 2 hours or until lamb is very tender. Add bread crumbs and cheese. Add beans and cook 30 minutes. Serve with extra cheese.

You can leave out the beans and serve over spaghetti. Fresh parsley and slivered lemon peel can be added at the end as a garnish.

This is a robust recipe, like a thick soup.

Jane Giorgiode
Columbus Ladies Auxiliary

LAMB CHOPS WITH ROSEMARY

1 tablespoon fresh rosemary	2 cloves garlic, crushed
½ tablespoon fresh sage or marjoram	2 tablespoons olive oil
	1 tablespoon lemon juice
6 lamb chops or lamb steaks	salt and pepper to taste

Crush up the rosemary and sage or marjoram and place in a bowl along with the lamb. Add the garlic and oil and allow to marinate for 3 hours or longer if your wish. Place the meat on a broiling rack, and broil, under high heat for about 5 minutes on each side or to your taste. Splash with the lemon juice, add salt and pepper, and serve hot.

Serve with broiled tomatoes, polenta and green salad.

Ana M. Zingarello
Raffaello Lodge #2661

VEAL SPEDINI TERMINI

1 pound veal, cut for spedini into 3-inch squares	6 sprigs parsley, chopped
2 (16 ounce) cans crushed tomatoes	1½ cups corn oil, divided
	¼ pound imported Fontina cheese, cut into 1-inch pieces
2 cups bread crumbs	
½ cup locatelli cheese or Parmesan cheese, grated	2 medium onions, sliced
	12 bay leaves

Marinate veal spedini in crushed tomatoes overnight or at least 2 hours before preparing. Combine bread crumbs with cheese and chopped parsley in a bowl. In a frying pan, put 1 cup oil and toast the bread crumb mixture until golden. Set aside to cool. Pour remaining ½ cup oil in bottom of a 13 x 9-inch baking dish, coating entire bottom of pan. Coat each spedini on both sides with toasted bread crumb mixture. Place 1 piece of Fontina cheese in center of spedini square. Overlap opposite sides over cheese. Place each spedini in baking dish with 1 onion slice and 1 bay leaf in rows. Spread remaining crushed tomatoes over spedini. Bake at 375° for 30 minutes. Don't overcook.

Mrs. Cuomo is pleased to share with you her favorite Italian recipe and extends her very best wishes for a memorable celebration.

Matilda Cuomo
Executive Mansion, Albany

STUFFED VEAL CUTLETS MARSALA

Stuffing:

1 (10 ounce) package chopped, frozen spinach (cooked, drained and cooled) (use only 6 ounces for stuffing)

7 fresh mushrooms, finely chopped

2 scallions, finely chopped

4 ounces shredded mozzarella cheese

1 sausage, cooked and finely chopped

2 cloves garlic, minced

Sauce:

1 large onion, sliced

2 scallions, chopped

8 ounces fresh mushrooms, sliced

1 red bell pepper, sliced

3 cloves garlic, chopped

1 cooked sausage, chopped

4 ounces cooked spinach

1½ cups crushed tomatoes

½ cup Marsala wine

¼ cup chicken broth

chopped fresh basil

chopped fresh bay leaves

salt and ground pepper to taste

Pound 1½ pounds of veal cutlets with mallet until each slice is flat and thin. Mix ingredients for stuffing and place on top of each veal cutlet and fold closed. Dip stuffed veal cutlets in flour, then beaten eggs, then bread crumbs. Place oil and butter in a large skillet and fry stuffed veal cutlets.

To prepare sauce, use another large skillet to sauté onions, scallions, mushrooms, red bell pepper and garlic in oil and butter. Add crushed tomatoes, wine, chicken broth, basil, bay leaves, salt and ground pepper. Cover and simmer 20 minutes. Pour sauce over meat. Sprinkle 2 ounces shredded mozzarella and cover and simmer for 15 to 20 minutes. Garnish with fresh parsley and serve.
Serves 4.

Madeline Matteucci
John A. Prudenti Lodge #2442

VEAL SCALOPPINE WITH PEPPERS AND MUSHROOMS

1 pound veal steak (½-inch
   thick)
½ cup flour
¾ tablespoon msg
½ teaspoon salt
⅛ teaspoon pepper
¼ cup olive oil
½ pound fresh mushrooms

1⅓ cups tomatoes
¼ teaspoon chopped parsley
¼ teaspoon oregano
1 clove garlic
1 green pepper
2 tablespoons butter or
   margarine

Pound veal, cut ½-inch thick, cut veal into 1-inch pieces. Combine in plastic bag, flour, msg, salt and pepper. Coat veal by shaking 2 or 3 pieces in plastic bag mixture. Set aside. Heat skillet, oil, and garlic until garlic is slightly brown. Add veal, slowly brown on both sides. While browning, in a bowl combine tomatoes, salt, parsley, oregano and black pepper. Slowly add mixture to browned veal. Cover and simmer for 25 minutes. Brown mushrooms and green pepper in butter or margarine until brown. Combine to veal and tomato mixture.
Serves 3 to 4.

Teena Spera
Constantino Brumidi Ladies Auxiliary

VEAL ZUCCHINI STEW

1½ pounds veal stew meat
1 medium onion
2 stalks of celery
1 package mushrooms
2 fresh tomatoes
1 large zucchini

1 large yellow squash
3 carrots
3 small potatoes
fresh parsley
salt and pepper

Brown veal dipped in flour, brown onion, celery and mushrooms. Place in large 6-quart pot. Add tomatoes, quartered; add potatoes, carrots, parsley, all cut and diced; add 1 cup water and simmer. After 1½ hours add zucchini and summer squash. Cook another hour or until veal is tender. Season with salt and pepper to taste.
Serves 6.

Marilyn A. Aragosa
Gabriele D'Annunzio Lodge #321

VEAL SCALOPPINE PICCATA

1½ or 2 pounds veal cut from the leg or the fillet
¼ cup all-purpose flour
6 tablespoons fresh creamery butter
½ teaspoon salt
¼ teaspoon freshly ground black pepper
juice of 1½ fresh lemons
10 fresh parsley sprigs, leaves only, chopped fine

Cut the veal into ½-inch slices and pound very thin. Dip the veal slices into the flour, shaking off any excess. Place the butter in a large skillet and heat. Add the veal and brown on both sides on high heat. Add salt and pepper and cook for about 5 minutes. Shake the skillet. Add lemon juice and parsley and cook for 1 minute. Arrange on hot plates and spoon the sauce over the veal. This dish goes well with mashed potatoes.
Serves 4.

Frances C. Brocchi
Aquileia Ladies Lodge #935

OSSO BUCO

4 veal shanks
3 tablespoons flour
1 onion, minced
1 clove garlic, minced
2 small carrots, chopped
1 small stalk celery, chopped
1 (28 ounce) can chopped whole tomatoes
2 bay leaves
1 cup dry white wine
salt and pepper to taste
¼ cup chopped parsley
grated lemon peel

Coat 4 pieces of veal shanks with flour. Heat ½ cup cooking oil in heavy skillet. Add minced garlic clove, add shanks and brown on both sides. Add chopped onion, carrots, celery, tomatoes, bay leaves and wine. Cover and cook slowly 1½ to 2 hours.

Add salt and pepper to taste. Sprinkle with chopped parsley and grated lemon peel. Serve with rice or spaghetti.
Yield: 4 servings.

Rosalie Galatioto
Giovanni Caboto Lodge #2372

BRACCIOLINI DI VITELLO

(Veal Rollettes)

1 (1¾ ounce) can anchovy fillets	8 slices provolone cheese
¼ cup milk	4 tablespoons margarine or butter
8 veal cutlets, ⅛-inch thick	1 tablespoon chopped parsley
8 slices prosciutto or ham	1 tablespoon lemon juice

Soak anchovies in milk for 15 minutes to remove excess salt; rinse, dry on paper towel. On each slice of veal, place 1 slice of prosciutto, 1 slice of cheese and 2 anchovies. Roll and fasten with toothpicks. Melt margarine in a large skillet. Brown veal rolls on all sides in margarine. Stir in parsley and lemon juice. Cook over medium heat, basting rolls frequently, until veal is cooked, about 12 to 15 minutes.
Makes 6 to 8 servings.

Catherine A. Perry
Geneva American Italian Ladies Lodge #2397A

STUFFED CALAMARI

12 medium squid tubes	pepper to taste
3 eggs, beaten	2 cups flavored bread crumbs
¼ cup fresh parsley, chopped	1 quart marinara sauce,
1 teaspoon salt, or to taste	partially cooked

Mix beaten eggs, parsley, garlic powder, salt, pepper and bread crumbs in a large bowl. Hold squid tube open and insert a teaspoon of bread crumb mixture. Use a toothpick to seal open end. When all the squid has been stuffed, sauté in lightly greased pan for approximately 2 minutes, turning every 30 seconds. Remove from pan and add to marinara sauce. Cook over medium heat for 20 to 25 minutes.
Serves 4.

Preparation time: 30 to 40 minutes.

Lucy Delio
Guy Lombardo Lodge #2417

CALAMARI (FRIED)

3 pounds cleaned squid
(cut in circles or rings)
2 eggs
1 teaspoon salt
1 teaspoon pepper

1 garlic clove, minced,
in olive oil
1 cup flour
1 (12 ounce) can beer

Cut squid in 1-inch rings. Combine eggs, beer, flour, onion, garlic, salt and pepper. Dip small handful of squid circles in flour and egg batter. Deep fry in hot oil until golden brown. Remove with slotted spoon and drain on paper towel.

Serve with cocktail sauce or hot marinara sauce.

Connie Conte
Enrico Caruso Lodge #2663

BAKED BLUE FISH

1 large, whole blue fish,
cleaned
3 lemons
fresh parsley

salt and pepper to taste
3 tablespoons olive oil
2-3 cloves fresh garlic, chopped

Lay blue fish flat in baking pan. Make diagonal slits down fish. Place garlic and fresh parsley into slits. In bowl, squeeze lemons and mix with olive oil. Place pan in oven at 400°. Bake for ½ hour. Remove pan and pour liquid mixture on fish. Put back under broiler and finish cooking until tan in color.

Jean Pisculli
Andrea Doria Lodge #2201

STUFFED FLOUNDER WITH CRAB MEAT

6 pan-dressed flounder, fresh
or frozen (or 6 flounder
filet)
3 cans crab meat
½ cup finely chopped onion
⅓ cup finely chopped celery
⅓ cup chopped green pepper
1 or 2 cloves of garlic, finely
chopped

2 cups soft bread cubes
3 beaten eggs
1 tablespoon chopped parsley
2 teaspoons salt
½ teaspoon pepper
⅓ cup lemon juice
¾ cup melted margarine

To serve 6, have 6 pan-dressed flounder. Thaw frozen fish. Clean, wash and dry. Put the fish on a cutting board, light side down. With a sharp knife cut down the center along the backbone from the tail to about 1 inch from the head end. Turn the knife flat and cut the flesh along both sides of the backbone to the tail, allowing the knife to run over the rib bone.

For stuffing, drain 3 cans crab meat, removing any shell or cartilage. Cook onion, celery, green pepper and garlic in ⅓ cup oil until tender. Combine soft bread cubes, beaten eggs, parsley, salt and pepper, cooked vegetables and the crab meat. Mix thoroughly. Stuff fish loosely. (If using filet, place stuffing on center of filet, fold over and use toothpicks to secure).

Combine ¾ cup melted margarine, ½ cup lemon juice and salt. Cut 6 pieces of heavy-duty Alcoa wrap, about 18 inches square. Grease lightly. Place 2 teaspoons of lemon sauce on foil. Place fish in sauce. Top each fish with 1 tablespoon of sauce and sprinkle with paprika. Bring the foil up over the fish and close all edges with tight double folds. Make 6 packages. Place packages on grill about 6 inches from moderately hot coals. Cook approximately 10 minutes or until fish flakes easily when tested with a fork. Can also bake fish in oven at 350° for approximately ½ hour, or until fish flakes easily when tested with a fork.
Serves 6.

Frances C. Brocchi
Aquileia Ladies Lodge #935

FILET OF SOLE PIZZAIOLA

1 pound filet of sole
1 tablespoon oregano
1 tablespoon chopped parsley
juice of 1 lemon

½ cup of bread crumbs
½ cup canned plum tomatoes
salt and pepper to taste
¼ cup olive oil

Blend thoroughly bread crumbs, oregano, parsley, salt and pepper. Roll fish in this mixture.

Put half of oil in baking dish; place breaded filet in dish. Spread tomatoes over fish; pour balance of oil over it. Bake in 375° oven for 20 minutes or until tender. Serve immediately with lemon juice.
Serves 4.

Lucy F. Codella
Aquileia Ladies Lodge #935

DRY COD FLORENTINE

(Baccala Fiorentina)

2 pounds dry cod fish
2 cloves garlic
4 tablespoons tomato paste
2 sprigs fresh parsley
1 tablespoon capers, washed

½ cup olive oil
½ cup flour
1 cup warm water
pinch of pepper to taste or
   dash of red crushed pepper

Soak cod fish in cold water for 24 hours. Change water several times. Wash in cold water before cooking. Cut fish in 4-inch serving pieces.

Roll in flour. Heat oil in skillet. Brown garlic 3 minutes. Fry fish about 3 to 4 minutes on each side until light brown. Sprinkle lightly with pepper to taste.

Blend tomato paste with warm water and pour over fish, add parsley and capers. Cover and simmer about 10 to 15 minutes until tender and well done. Serve very hot.
Serves 4.

Joseph E. Fay
Santa Rosalia Lodge #2131

FRESH TUNA—SICILIAN STYLE

4 (¾-inch) fresh tuna steaks
½ cup olive oil
¼ cup wine vinegar

2 medium-size onions, sliced
flour, salt and pepper

Wash and dry tuna. Coat tuna with seasoned flour. Heat oil in frying pan on medium heat. When oil is hot, place tuna in pan. Fry until golden brown on both sides. Remove tuna from pan and set aside.

In same oil cook onions until transparent, add vinegar and simmer for 2 to 3 minutes. Return tuna to pan (onion still in pan) and cook for 1 minute, turning once.

Place tuna on a platter and pour onion mixture on top. Garnish with fresh basil or fresh mint. Serve at room temperature or cold.
Serves 2.

Nancy Romano
Giovanni Caboto Lodge #2372

STUFFED FILLET OF SOLE— ITALIAN STYLE

8 fillets of sole
½ cup Monterey Jack or
    Cheddar cheese, cubed
¼ cup cottage cheese or ricotta
    cheese
¾ cup plain bread crumbs

½ cup crab meat, flaked
2 tablespoons minced garlic
2 tablespoons chopped parsley
1 egg
salt and pepper to taste

Lemon Butter Sauce:
¼ cup butter or margarine
1 tablespoon lemon juice

1 tablespoon white wine

Mix all ingredients except fillets. Put filling on one fillet and cover with second fillet. With sharp knife, make 3 slits diagonally on top fillet. Brush with melted butter or margarine. Bake 25 minutes at 375° or broil 10 minute, 8 inches from flame.

Lemon Butter Sauce: Heat butter or margarine, lemon juice and wine. Pour over fish just before serving.
Serves 4.

Phyllis Ventimiglia
Italo Balbo Lodge #2361

KING SHRIMP PROVENÇALE

1 pound fresh large shrimp
3 peeled tomatoes
1 clove garlic
1 stalk celery
½ onion

paprika
salt and pepper to taste
¾ cup fresh bread crumbs
2 tablespoons butter

Peel and clean fresh shrimp and place in fireproof baking dish. Chop tomatoes, garlic, celery and onion. Sprinkle vegetable mixture over shrimp. Add paprika and salt and pepper to taste. Top with fresh bread crumbs and dot with butter. Bake at 375° for 20 minutes.

Sandy Bernardi
Per Sempre Ladies Lodge #2344A

SHRIMP PASCARELLA

30 small shrimp
1 tablespoon plus 1 teaspoon
    dried basil
2 tablespoons chopped green
    onion
8 black olives, sliced
⅛ teaspoon pepper

½ pound angel hair pasta
2½ cups chopped tomato
1 cup chunky tomato sauce
3 tablespoons white wine
⅛ teaspoon salt
⅛ teaspoon garlic powder

Combine chopped tomato, basil, tomato sauce, green onions, wine, olives, salt, pepper and garlic powder in large saucepan and simmer 8 to 12 minutes, stirring occasionally.

Remove tails from shrimp if desired. Cook pasta and drain well. Add shrimp to tomato mixture. Simmer until warm, about 4 minutes. Serve over pasta.

Erna Pascarella
William C. LaMorte Lodge #2251

117

SHRIMP MARINARA

½ cup oil
2 cloves garlic
1 large onion, chopped
1 (26 ounce) can whole
   tomatoes

2 tablespoons basil
2 tablespoons oregano
2 pounds large shrimp
   (cleaned and deveined)
salt and pepper to taste

In a saucepan, heat oil and garlic until garlic sizzles. Add chopped onion, whole tomatoes (crush them), oregano, basil and salt and pepper. Boil and then simmer about 30 minutes. Add shrimp and boil until tender. Simmer long enough to get shrimp hot, but don't overcook or your shrimp will be tough. Serve over freshly cooked linguine.

Tip: When boiling shrimp, add a squirt of lemon juice or a teaspoon of vinegar to the water to prevent kitchen odor.

Yvette Spisak
Daughters of Columbus Lodge #1666

SCALLOPS WITH GARLIC AND PARSLEY

1½ pounds bay or sea scallops
3 tablespoons flour
½ cup fresh chopped parsley
2 tablespoons butter

2 cloves garlic
2 tablespoons olive oil
lemon wedges

Wash scallops and drain thoroughly. If scallops are large, cut in half. Place flour seasoned with salt and pepper in bowl. Add scallops and using hands or spoon, coat with flour. Over medium heat, heat oil and butter until hot.

Mince garlic and cook 30 seconds. Add scallops in single layer in skillet and turn once until cooked through. Do not crowd. Add chopped parsley. The entire cooking time is 4 minutes. Remove scallops and serve with lemon wedges.

Pat Quatraro
Cellini Lodge #2206

SCALLOPS AND FETTUCCINE

1 large sweet onion, chopped
2 cloves garlic, minced
½ cup dry white wine, divided in 2 parts
1 (16 ounce) can plain tomato sauce
2 tablespoons fresh basil or 2 teaspoons dried basil
1 teaspoon fresh oregano or ½ teaspoon dried oregano
4 cups of tender cooked fettuccine or other pasta
2 large ripe tomatoes, peeled and cubed
1 pound scallops

Spray a large nonstick skillet or electric frying pan with cooking spray or olive oil. Add the onion, garlic and ¼ cup wine. Cook uncovered until wine evaporates and onion begins to brown.

Stir in tomato sauce and herbs, cover and simmer 15 to 20 minutes. Meanwhile, cook pasta in boiling salted water until tender. Uncover sauce and stir in remaining wine, tomatoes and scallops. Cook and stir 1 to 2 minutes, only until scallops are heated through. Spoon sauce over hot drained pasta.
Serves 4.

Laura DeSario
St. Francis of Assisi Lodge #2629

SCALLOPS, BROCCOLI RABE AND SPINACH

½ pound broccoli rabe, washed and trimmed
½ pound spinach, washed
1 tablespoon butter
3 tablespoons olive oil
18 large scallops
salt and pepper
½ cup good white wine
1 tablespoon balsamic vinegar

Steam broccoli rabe in a saucepan, 3 to 4 minutes. Remove from heat and drain. Steam spinach 3 to 4 minutes and drain. Chop greens, add butter, set aside and keep hot.

Heat oil in pan and sauté scallops for about 1½ minutes on each side. Add wine and vinegar and braise for 3 more minutes. Place warm greens on plate and arrange scallops on top. Drizzle juice on all.

Jo Truglio
Mario Lanza Lodge #2491

BAKED LOBSTER ITALIANO

4 lobster tails
2 tablespoons white wine
2 tablespoons water
3 tablespoons bread crumbs
1 tablespoon chopped parsley
2 tablespoons grated Parmesan
   cheese

1 teaspoon chopped basil
1 clove chopped garlic
4 tablespoons olive oil
small pinch wild marjoram
salt and pepper

Split lobster lengthwise. Place in a roasting pan, shell side down, and pour wine and water into pan. Mix bread crumbs with parsley, cheese, basil, garlic and marjoram. Sprinkle mixture over lobster tails. Season to taste with salt and pepper, baste with oil and bake for 20 minutes in a moderate 325° oven.

Imma Riccardelli
Guglielmo Marconi Ladies Auxiliary

AUNT ROSALIE'S SARDE MODIGA

12 fresh sardines (about 5
   inches long)
1 cup flavored bread crumbs,
   browned in oil over a low
   flame
½ cup chopped onion,
   browned

raisins
pignoli nuts (optional)
fresh bay leaves
onion pieces (approximately
   ¾-inch wide x 2 inches
   thick)

Lay sardines out flat and split almost through lengthwise. Stuff with mixture of bread crumbs, browned onion, raisins and nuts; close sardines and thread onto skewers alternately with bay leaf and onion pieces.

Oil bottom of pan. Lay skewers in pan. Bake at 350° for about ½ hour.

Marcy Dabbene
William C. LaMorte Lodge #2251

SARDE BECCAFICO
(Stuffed Fresh Sardines)

2 pounds large fresh sardines   marinara sauce

Clean carefully, slit down center to form an open filet and remove bones.

Stuffing:

1½ cups bread crumbs   1 clove garlic, chopped
2 tablespoons chopped parsley   4 tablespoons olive oil
¼ cup grated cheese   pepper to taste

Mix all ingredients thoroughly; add a little more oil if needed to make a firm mixture. Cover whole filet with stuffing, top with another filet to form a sandwich. Tie with white thread to keep stuffing in.

Place fish carefully into pan of marinara sauce. Cover, cook over low flame 15 minutes or until fish is tender. Remove fish carefully and place on flat dish or platter. Cut threads and remove. Pour sauce over spaghetti.

Veronica Martino
William C. LaMorte Lodge #2251

FISH STEAK A LA MARINARA

2 pounds fish steak (cod or   ½ teaspoon pepper
    halibut steaks)   ¼ cup chopped green olives
2 cups strained cooked   2 tablespoons capers
    tomatoes (#2 can)   1 teaspoon salt
1 tablespoon chopped parsley   ½ teaspoon oregano

Grease a 1½-quart casserole. Wipe with clean damp cloth. Place steaks in pan and set aside.

In a separate saucepan combine the above ingredients and bring to a boil. Pour mixture over fish steaks. Bake at 350° for 25 to 30 minutes or until fish flakes easily.
Serves 4.

Antonio P. Baffo
Marcus Aurelius Lodge #2321

BAKED FISH WITH FETA CHEESE

4 pounds fish fillets
  (whitefish, bass or halibut)
4 fresh tomatoes, peeled and
  sliced
1 cup white wine
2 tablespoons chopped parsley
¾ cup olive oil

1 clove garlic, crushed
1 teaspoon basil
1 cup bread crumbs
1 slice feta cheese for each slice
  of fish
salt and pepper to taste

Place fillets in a baking dish. In a separate bowl, combine tomatoes, olive oil, wine, parsley, garlic, basil, salt and pepper. Pour over fish fillets. Sprinkle with bread crumbs. Set oven at 350° and bake 40 minutes. Top fillets with feta cheese and broil 1 or 2 minutes.
Makes 6 to 8 servings.

Lucille Baffo
Marcus Aurelius Lodge #2321

BAKED RED SNAPPER

8 ounces boned red snapper
  fillet
1 medium onion, sliced
1 fennel bulb, sliced
1 tablespoon oregano
1 tablespoon parsley

4 ounces chicken stock
2 ounces dry white wine
1½ tablespoons butter
1 tablespoon garlic, chopped
½ pound fresh spinach, raw
salt and pepper to taste

Score back of red snapper fillet. Place skin side down on a bed of fresh spinach. Add sliced onion and fennel and mixture of remaining ingredients over fish. Bake at 400° for 10 to 15 minutes.

Serve with roasted red potatoes and vegetable of choice.

Robert Albertson
Arturo Toscanini Lodge #2107

GRILLED FISH

4 salmon, shark, tuna, or other
    firm fish steaks
2 large vine-ripe tomatoes,
    sliced
1 large onion, sliced
16 large asparagus spears

¼ cup chopped Italian parsley
¼ cup melted butter
1 tablespoon lemon juice
8 large basil leaves
½ teaspoon dill

Marinade ingredients:
½ teaspoon ground ginger
½ cup extra virgin olive oil
⅛ cup soy or teriyaki sauce
3 scallions, chopped
1 shallot, finely chopped

5 cloves crushed garlic
⅛ cup white wine
juice of 1 lemon
½ teaspoon fresh ground
    pepper

Mix all marinade ingredients, pour half over fish and let soak until fish begins to change color, but no longer than 20 minutes. Place fish on grill over low flame, or on oven broiler at 275°. Baste fish frequently. When fish are half done, grill or broil tomato and onion slices and lightly baste them. Grill asparagus spears, but do not baste them. When fish and vegetables are fully cooked, arrange tomato slices and onion slices on a plate with 1 tablespoon of marinade, place basil leaves on top, then place cooked fish on top of the basil leaves. Arrange asparagus spears to the side, and cover in lemon, butter, and dill. Douse fish lightly with marinade and serve.

Joanne Randazza
Gloucester, Massachusetts

CASTELFORTESE CHICKEN

1 or 2 spring chickens	2-3 cloves garlic, minced
olive oil	juice of 1 whole lemon
parsley, basil, mint (fresh if possible, if not 1 teaspoon to taste)	peas (fresh, frozen or canned) 1 package frozen artichoke hearts
1 small onion, minced	white wine (optional)

Cut 1 or 2 spring chickens into small pieces. Soak in salted water a few minutes then rinse and pat dry.

Marinate in a little olive oil, parsley, basil, mint, 1 small minced onion, 2 to 3 cloves minced garlic and juice of one whole lemon. Toss well and marinate at least 2 hours.

Remove chicken and brown in hot oil in frying pan. Remove to baking pan and place in 350° oven and bake 15 minutes.

To the marinade that is left from the chicken, add fresh, frozen or canned peas and a package of frozen artichoke hearts and heat in frying pan after chicken is removed.

Add marinade to chicken in oven and continue baking until well browned. Add salt and pepper to taste. Also add white wine if desired.

This recipe can be made with any chicken parts or just breasts.

This recipe is from the Province of Latina, which is located on the central Western Coast of Italy, sandwiched between Rome and Naples.

Diane Parente
Giovanni Caboto Lodge #2372

POLLO ARROSTO IN PADELLA

(Pan Roasted Chicken)

1 (2½-3½ pound) frying chicken, cut into serving pieces
2 tablespoons butter
2 tablespoons olive oil
3 garlic cloves, crushed

2 sprigs fresh rosemary or 1 teaspoon dried rosemary
salt and freshly ground pepper to taste
½ cup dry white wine

Wash and dry chicken thoroughly. Melt butter with oil in a large skillet. When butter foams, add chicken pieces, garlic and rosemary. Brown chicken on all sides over medium heat. Season with salt and pepper. Add wine. When wine is reduced by half, partially cover skillet. Cook over medium heat 30 to 40 minutes or until chicken is tender.

Place chicken on a warm platter. If sauce looks dry, stir in a little more wine. If sauce is too thin, increase heat and boil uncovered until it reaches desired thickness. Remove most of the fat from sauce. Taste and adjust sauce with seasoning, then spoon over chicken. Serve immediately.

Makes 4 servings.

Pan roasting is typically Italian and helps meat to retain its moisture.

Catherine A. Perry
Geneva American Italian Ladies Lodge #2397A

CHICKEN WITH ROASTED PEPPERS

2 whole chickens
1 small can of tomato paste
1 large jar of roasted peppers
1 jar of black cured Sicilian
    olives, pitted and cut up

2 cloves garlic, minced
oregano
salt and pepper to taste
red pepper flakes, optional

Boil 2 whole chickens. Skin, bone and then shred chickens. Add garlic, red pepper flakes (optional), salt, black pepper and oregano. Add 1 small can of tomato paste, 1 large jar of roasted peppers (sliced into strips), and black cured Sicilian olives. Mix thoroughly and heat in large frying pan with a little oil until thoroughly mixed and heated.

Great for hero sandwiches.

Rosalie Galatioto
Giovanni Caboto Lodge #2372

CHICKEN SPITSADE

1 whole chicken
3-4 cloves garlic
parsley

salt and pepper
1 cup white wine
1 teaspoon rosemary

Cut chicken into small pieces. Sauté garlic in oil; remove. Brown chicken in oil a few pieces at a time. Remove to a dish that has a cover.

After all the chicken has been browned and removed, empty some of the oil out of the frying pan. Leave a little. To this add about a cup of white wine, some salt and pepper and about 1 teaspoon or a little more of rosemary. Bring this to a boil. Stir all drippings in the pan (it cleans the pan good.) Pour this over the chicken in the covered dish. Steam for approximately 45 minutes to 1 hour.

You can marinate the chicken first in oil, parsley, salt and pepper then proceed with the frying, etc.

Suggested accompaniments with the chicken are: Noodles or rice, a vegetable and tossed salad.

Donald DiRito
Christopher Columbus Lodge #692

CHICKEN CACCIATORE I

2 pounds skinless chicken
14 ounces crushed tomatoes
1 medium onion, chopped
handful chopped parsley

¼ cup oil
oregano to taste
salt to taste
5-6 capers

Mix all ingredients in large bowl and bake in baking pan at 400° for about 1 hour.

Francesca Fratto
Raffaello Lodge #2661

CHICKEN CACCIATORE II

2 chickens, remove skin and
　cut in pieces
1 onion, diced
1 can caponata (eggplant
　appetizer)
1 (16 ounce) can crushed
　tomatoes

¼ cup red wine
salt and pepper to taste
olive oil
fresh parsley, chopped
fresh basil, whole or chopped

Wash chicken and drain. In saucepan fry chicken in just enough oil to cover bottom of pan. Salt and pepper each piece on both sides before frying, turning each piece until well done and brown. Remove from pan. In same pan, brown onions until well done. Add crushed tomatoes, caponata, wine, parsley, basil and salt and pepper to taste. Mix well and lower heat.

Mix chicken in sauce well, and cook for about 1 hour on low heat with cover on pot slightly tilted. Stir frequently so mixture will not stick to bottom of pan. Serve over spaghetti.

Jean Pisculli
Andrea Doria Lodge #2201

SOPHIE'S ITALIAN STYLE BARBECUED CHICKEN

3-3½ pounds chicken
flour, salt and pepper
2 tablespoons shortening
1 medium onion, sliced
1 clove garlic, finely minced
1 teaspoon salt
¼ teaspoon pepper
¼ teaspoon dry mustard

1 tablespoon Worcestershire
  sauce
1 bay leaf
¼ cup vinegar
1 teaspoon sugar
1 tablespoon brown sugar
1½ cups tomato sauce

Cut chicken in serving pieces and dredge in seasoned flour. Preheat fry pan at 350°. Melt shortening and fry chicken until golden brown.

Combine onion, garlic, salt, pepper, mustard, Worcestershire sauce, bay leaf, vinegar, sugar, brown sugar and tomato sauce and pour over chicken. Reduce heat to 250°. Cover and cook until tender and well done, adding water if necessary. Remove bay leaf before serving.

Sophie Sciame
Cellini Lodge #2206

CHICKEN AND ARTICHOKES

1 large frying chicken, cut up
2 tablespoons olive oil
1 small onion, chopped
1 clove garlic, minced
1 teaspoon flour
1 cup hot chicken broth
1 tablespoon tomato paste

¼ cup chopped fresh parsley
1 teaspoon dried rosemary
1 teaspoon salt
¼ teaspoon pepper
6 fresh artichokes, cleaned and
  cut in half
1 cup white wine

In large skillet, brown chicken in oil. Transfer chicken to large baking pan. Brown onion and garlic in remaining oil. Slowly stir in flour and add broth, tomato paste and seasoning. Add artichoke halves to sauce and simmer 5 minutes. Add wine and simmer 2 to 3 minutes.

Arrange artichokes and chicken alternately in baking pan. Pour sauce over all. Bake at 325° until tender, about 1 hour. Serve.

Olga V. Pacil
Geneva American Italian Ladies Lodge #2397A

PARMESAN CHICKEN

4 half boneless, skinned
   chicken breast
6 tablespoons grated Parmesan
   cheese
1 tablespoon grated Parmesan
   cheese

1 tablespoon flour
½ cup onions, finely chopped
4 tablespoons olive oil
1 cup sliced mushrooms
1 can stewed tomatoes

Flatten chicken slightly with mallet. Coat chicken with Parmesan cheese and then the flour. In a skillet cook chicken in 2 tablespoons of oil over medium heat until golden. Remove them to a serving dish. In skillet add the rest of oil, mushrooms and onions until they are soft; add tomatoes and cook until thickened. Spoon over chicken and sprinkle cheese. (1 tablespoon)

Filomena Mastria
Raffaello Lodge #2661

CHICKEN PICCATA

4 boneless chicken breasts, cut
   in half and lightly pounded
flour for dredging
3 tablespoons butter
1 cup white wine

2 cups chicken stock
2 tablespoons lemon juice
salt, pepper and chopped
   parsley

Flour the chicken breasts. In a large sauté pan, melt butter, brown the chicken on both sides. Add the white wine, chicken stock, lemon juice, salt and pepper. Simmer chicken until the sauce thickens. This will take about 5 to 7 minutes. Toss in parsley and serve.

Louise DeLisio
Le Amiche Lodge #2550

CHICKEN SCARPARIELLO

10 ounces skinned and boned
   chicken breasts cut in strips
   (1 x 3 inches)
3 tablespoons all-purpose flour
2 teaspoons each vegetable oil
   and margarine
2 tablespoons minced shallots
   or onion
2 cloves garlic, minced

1 cup water
½ cup dry white table wine
1 packet instant chicken broth
½ teaspoon ground rosemary
   leaves
¼ teaspoon salt
dash pepper
1 tablespoon chopped chives

On a sheet of wax paper or a paper plate dredge chicken in flour.

In a 10-inch nonstick skillet combine oil and margarine and heat over medium-high heat until margarine is bubbly and hot. Add chicken and cook, turning occasionally, until lightly browned on all sides, 3 to 4 minutes. Using tongs or slotted spoon, remove chicken from skillet and set aside.

To the same skillet add shallots, (or onion) and garlic and sauté until softened, about one minute. Add water, wine, broth mix and seasoning. Using a wooden spoon, stir well. Cook, stirring frequently, until liquid is reduced by half (3 to 4 minutes). Return chicken to skillet and cook until sauce is thick and chicken is heated through, 1 to 2 minutes. Serve sprinkled with chives.
Serves 2.

Pat Quatraro
Cellini Lodge #2206

CHICKEN LINGUANTI

1 (2-3 pound) frying chicken
   (cut into pieces) or 4 legs
   and 4 thighs or 4 breasts

1 (8 ounce) bottle Zesty Italian
   salad dressing
⅓ cup lemon juice

Marinate chicken in salad dressing and lemon juice in roasting pan.

In a 350° oven, bake for approximately 1 to 1½ hours or until golden brown. (Do not remove skin from chicken until after it has been cooked so as to keep the chicken moist.)

Paul W. Ludwig, Jr.
Vincent Linguanti Lodge #2212

CHICKEN A LA MARTINO

2 onions
2 peppers
2 tomatoes

4 chicken breasts, sliced
6 slices of cheese (mozzarella, Swiss-Lorraine, etc.)

Sauté onions and peppers; add tomatoes cut in wedges and cook for 8 minutes. Place sliced chicken breasts on top and simmer until white. Place cheese of your choice over chicken and simmer until cheese melts. Serve over a bed of rice.
Serves 4 to 6 people.

William Martino
Anthony Casamento Lodge #2612

CHICKEN WITH ARTICHOKE SAUCE

½ cup butter or margarine
½ cup olive oil
2 tablespoons flour
2 cups chicken broth
4 tablespoons capers, drained
1 can artichoke hearts, drained and sliced
1-2 cloves garlic, minced
2 tablespoons parsley

3-4 teaspoons fresh lemon juice
4 tablespoons Parmesan cheese
5 slices prosciutto, cut up (optional)
½ cup white wine
1 pound linguine or angel hair pasta
4-5 chicken breasts
salt and pepper to taste

Melt butter and olive oil in saucepan over medium heat. Add flour and stir until smooth, approximately 3 minutes. Blend in broth and stir until thickened. Reduce heat to low. Add garlic, parsley, lemon juice, salt and pepper. Cook 5 minutes (keep stirring). Blend in artichokes, cheese, capers, prosciutto and wine. Cover and simmer 8 minutes.

Flour chicken breasts and pan fry.

Cook pasta and drain. Place pasta in platter and add enough sauce to moisten. Top with chicken breasts and spoon remaining sauce over chicken and pasta.
Yield: Serves 4 to 5 people.

Michael Bologna
Mario Lanza Lodge #2491

CHICKEN A LA AMARETTO

2 chicken breasts sliced into 4
   cutlets
1 cup flour
1 egg, beaten
¼ cup oil

⅛ teaspoon salt
⅛ teaspoon pepper
1 orange
½ cup Amaretto
beef stock, see below

After slicing breasts, lightly pound. Dip into flour and egg.

Pour ¼ cup oil in frying pan and heat. Brown chicken lightly. Drain oil out of pan and put chicken back in pan.

Lower flame and add Amaretto, salt and pepper. Cut orange in half, squeeze juice of both halves into frying pan and add ½ cup of beef stock. Let simmer 3 minutes, turn cutlets over for 2 more minutes. Remove cutlets from pan. Allow gravy to simmer 3 to 4 minutes more.

Place chicken cutlets on dish. Pour gravy over dish, orange twist on top.

Beef stock: Melt ¼ stick of butter, add sifted flour and stir until thick. Add beef stock, ¾ cup Marsala wine and ⅛ teaspoon black pepper.

Ann Riccardi
Per Sempre Ladies Lodge #2344A

FRANK'S SUPER CHICKEN

1 pound chicken cutlets
1 egg
½ cup milk
1 can mushroom soup
cooking oil for frying

1 cup flour
8 ounces mozzarella cheese,
   sliced
salt and pepper to taste
6 ounces mushrooms, sliced

Mix flour, egg, milk, salt and pepper (to taste) to the thickness of pancake batter; add more or less milk for consistency. Prepare cutlets, dip into batter. Fry until golden brown.

Place 1 layer of cutlet into baking pan. Pour mushroom soup over cutlets. Place 1 slice of mozzarella on each cutlet. Top with mushrooms and bake until cheese melts.

Frank Ferrante
Constantino Brumidi Lodge #2211

CHICKEN AND VEGETABLES— ITALIAN STYLE

4 chicken cutlets	½ teaspoon oregano
4 medium-size green peppers	4 large tomatoes
4 large fresh mushrooms	½ teaspoon garlic powder
1 large onion	aluminum foil
salt and pepper to taste	

Place chicken cutlet on a piece of aluminum foil large enough to close. Slice tomatoes and green peppers into chunks. Slice mushrooms and onion into slices. Add seasoning. Wrap in tin foil. Place in baking dish, cook at 350° for ½ hour.

Make each of the 4 chicken cutlets the same way.

Teena Spera
Constantino Brumidi Ladies Auxiliary

CHICKEN ITELIENE

1 pound boneless chicken cutlets (cut in 1-inch cubes)	1 teaspoon minced garlic
1 tablespoon all-purpose flour	3 tablespoons olive oil
½ teaspoon pepper	1 (29 ounce) can tomato sauce
½ cup chopped fresh basil	¼ cup Parmesan cheese

In bowl, toss chicken with flour and pepper to coat. In large saucepan, sauté chicken with ¼ cup basil, onion and garlic in hot oil until chicken is fully cooked (no longer pink). Stir in tomato sauce and ¼ cup Parmesan cheese. Simmer, stirring occasionally uncovered for 30 minutes or until thickens. Serve sauce over pasta and sprinkle with additional Parmesan cheese if desired.
Makes 5 cups sauce.

Cathy Lloyd
Le Amiche Lodge #2550

EASY BAKED CHICKEN CUTLETS

3 or 4 fresh chicken cutlets,
  1-inch thick
1 clove garlic, chopped
1 tablespoon fresh parsley,
  chopped

½ cup seasoned bread crumbs
½ cup wine vinegar or
  balsamic vinegar
1 tablespoon semi-hot paprika

Wash and pat dry chicken cutlets. Place in a shallow glass baking dish and pour the vinegar over the cutlets. Sprinkle with bread crumbs. Add garlic, parsley and hot paprika and a little oil. Add ½ cup water and bake uncovered for 20 minutes at 400°.

Submitted by Felicity
Joseph E. Fay
Santa Rosalia Lodge #2131

CHICKEN LIVERS WITH SAGE

1 pound chicken livers
salt
freshly ground pepper
12-15 fresh sage leaves,
  chopped, or 1-2 tablespoons
  dried sage

4 tablespoons (¼ cup) butter
¼ cup minced prosciutto (or 2
  slices of bacon, minced)
¼ cup dry white wine

Trim chicken livers; if large, cut into halves. Season with salt and pepper and sprinkle with the sage. Heat butter and prosciutto in frying pan. Cook the livers in the pan over moderate heat, stirring frequently, for about 5 minutes or until browned. Add wine and simmer for 2 to 3 minutes longer.

Camille Codella
Aquileia Ladies Lodge #935

INSALATE E CONTORNI
SALADS AND VEGETABLES

NEW YORK OSIA FILIAL LODGES

• **America Lodge #2245**, West Hempstead, Charter issued 1971: America, the lands of the Western Hemisphere ... derived from the Florentine navigator, Amerigo Vespucci.

• **Joe Di Maggio Lodge #2248**, E. Fishkill, Charter issued 1971: Joseph Paul DiMaggio played baseball for the great New York Yankees. He rose to national fame and was admired and respected by millions for his baseball ability and his exemplary conduct on and off the field. "The Yankee Clipper" hit safely in 56 consecutive games and was inducted into the Baseball Hall of Fame in 1955.

• **William C. La Morte Lodge #2251**, Staten Island, Charter issued 1971: The Staten Island Lodge #2251 changed its name to the William C. LaMorte Lodge in honor of a well respected Staten Island civic and business leader. He served his country honorably with General Patton's 5th Army in World War II.

• **Anthony E. Terino Lodge #2252**, Mastic Beach, Charter issued 1972: Dr. Terino is an admired and respected educator known throughout New York State. He gained the highest career position in the New York State Education Department, namely, Director of the Division of School Supervision.

• **Galileo Galilei Lodge #2253**, Hicksville, Charter issued 1972: Galileo Galilei was a great scientist and astronomer and invented the first practical telescope. His detailed study of motion and method of expressing natural events mathematically opened the way to Isaac Newton's discovery of universal gravitation. Galileo served as a Professor of Mathematics at the University of Padua and University of Pisa.

• **Business & Professional Lodge #2269**, Flushing, Charter issued 1972: This lodge is composed of business and professional members in the Flushing area of Queens.

• **Vincent Lombardi Lodge #2270**, Rochester, Charter issued 1972: Considered one of the greatest football coaches of all time, Vincent Lombardi was inducted into the Football Hall of Fame in 1971. His philosophy was "winning isn't everything, it's the only thing!".

• **Bishop Pernicone Lodge #2313**, The Bronx, Charter issued 1974: Joseph M. Pernicone was the first Italian American bishop of the Archdiocese of New York.

• **Dr. Vincenzo Sellaro Lodge #2319**, Smithtown, Charter issued 1974: This lodge was named after the Founder of the Order Sons of Italy in America, Dr. Vincenzo Sellaro. The Order was founded in New York City on June 22, 1905.

• **Anthony Maggiacomo Lodge #2320**, Yonkers, Charter issued 1974: This lodge was named after the prominent Yonkers community activist, Anthony Maggiacomo.

• **Marcus Aurelius Lodge #2321**, Flushing, Charter issued 1974: Marcus Aurelius was born Marcus Annius Verus in Rome in 121 A.D. to a noble family. He is most famous for his "Meditations", which may best be described as a diary of philosophical reflections containing his own rules for living and the acceptance of life's difficulties.

• **Antoinette Vigilante Lodge #2329**, Brooklyn, Charter issued 1975: Named after an early woman activist and mother of the first Venerable of the lodge, Inez Fonti. Her son, John A. Vigilante of Connecticut, was National First Assistant Supreme Venerable.

(Continued on next divider page)

EGGS AND TOMATO A LA CARRERA

1 tablespoon olive oil
3 large eggs
10 leaves fresh basil

3 medium to large plum
   tomatoes
salt to taste

Add 1 tablespoon of olive oil to a medium frying pan. Heat oil at medium temperature.

Cut 3 plum tomatoes into quarters and crush them. (Hint: Try not to take out the seeds.) Place them into the hot oil.

Clean 10 leaves of basil and chop them up to the size of a dime, and place them in the pan with tomatoes.

Stir them together until the skin of the tomatoes peels off. Then place the eggs in the mixture sunny side up. Cover the frying pan and simmer at low heat. Cook until eggs are white on top. Serve when hot and ready.

Michael Carrera
Loggia Glen Cove #1016

STRING BEAN SALAD

string beans, fresh or frozen
4 cloves of garlic
1 tablespoon fresh mint (dry
   mint may be used)

wine vinegar
olive oil

Clean and cut string beans (or use frozen ones) and boil. Remove from heat, drain and cool under running water. Fully drain and then place them in a bowl. Cut up 4 cloves of garlic, and cut up 1 tablespoon of fresh mint. Add these and wine vinegar to the bowl and stir. Leave in refrigerator overnight. When ready to serve, stir, add olive oil, and stir again.

Mary Spinelli Crescitelli
William C. LaMorte Lodge #2251

MOTHER'S MUSHROOM SALAD

2-8 ounce cans of mushrooms,
  or ¼ pound fresh
  mushrooms, chopped
1 can black olives, chopped
½ green pepper, chopped
2 tablespoons olive oil

1 tablespoon wine vinegar
½ teaspoon oregano
½ teaspoon black pepper
1 clove garlic, chopped fine
salt to taste

Mix all ingredients together several hours before serving.

Judy Taverne
Utica Lodge #2054

RICE SALAD

2 cups rice, cooked and cooled
½ pound cubed ham

½ pound hard mozzarella
  cheese
mayonnaise

Mix together with mayonnaise to taste. Let sit overnight in the refrigerator, and enjoy the next day.

Rosellina Algieri Maher
Antonio Meucci Lodge #213

CHICK PEA SALAD

2 cups chick peas
1 clove garlic, finely minced
¼ cup chopped scallions
1 ripe tomato, cut into bite-size
  wedges

¼ cup finely chopped parsley
2 tablespoons wine vinegar
½ cup olive oil
salt and pepper to taste

Drain the chick peas well. Pour them into a salad bowl. Add the garlic, scallions, tomato and parsley. Sprinkle with the vinegar and toss. Sprinkle with the oil, salt and pepper. Toss again. Let stand 1 hour.

Maria Cicciarella
Constantino Brumidi Ladies Auxiliary

SQUID SALAD

1 pound squid, cleaned
3 tablespoons olive oil
3 garlic cloves, finely chopped
pinch of hot pepper flakes
½ cup dry white wine
1¼ teaspoons salt
¼ teaspoon dried oregano
2 celery ribs, thinly sliced
1 small red onion, thinly sliced

1 red bell pepper, cored,
  seeded and thinly sliced
2 tablespoons chopped fresh
  parsley
2 tablespoons chopped fresh
  basil or 1 teaspoon dried
2 tablespoons red wine vinegar
1 tablespoon fresh lemon juice
½ teaspoon pepper
lemon wedges

Cut squid into thin ¼- to ½-inch circles. In a nonreactive large frying pan, heat 2 tablespoons olive oil over medium heat. Add garlic and hot pepper flakes and cook 30 seconds, or until garlic is fragrant but not brown. Immediately add squid to pan and cook, stirring frequently, 1 to 2 minutes until squid just turns pink. Add wine, ½ teaspoon salt, and oregano for 1 minute and remove from heat. Set aside and let cool.

In a large bowl, combine celery, red onion, bell pepper, parsley, basil, vinegar, lemon juice, pepper and remaining 1 tablespoon olive oil and mix. Add squid with its liquid and remaining ¾ teaspoon salt. Serve with lemon wedges.
Serves 4 to 6.

Gloria Enea
Utica Lodge #2054

INSALATA D'OLIVE

(Olive Salad)

1 can green olives, drained
1 can black olives, drained
1 cup celery, chopped
1 green pepper, chopped
1 sweet red pepper, chopped

2 cloves garlic, minced
¼ cup olive oil
¼ cup wine vinegar
½ teaspoon ground pepper
1 teaspoon oregano

Crush olives until pit shows and remove pits. Combine with remaining ingredients. Let stand at room temperature about 6 hours. Cover and refrigerate.
Serves 6.

Josephine Baldanza
Romanesque Lodge #2198

LENTIL BEAN SALAD

½ cup barley, cooked
1 pound lentils, cooked until firm, but tender
2 cups brown rice, cooked
1 can chick peas, rinsed and drained
1 can black beans, rinsed and drained

1 can red kidney beans, rinsed and drained
4 plum tomatoes, diced
1 small onion, diced
1 (16 ounce) bottle Italian diet dressing

Mix all together and enjoy!

Gloria Molinaro
Romanesque Lodge #2198

TOMATO, CHEESE AND BASIL SALAD

3 medium-sized tomatoes (ripe)
½ pound mozzarella cheese
fresh basil leaves, rinsed and well drained

1 small onion, chopped
2 tablespoons olive oil
2 teaspoons wine vinegar
1 loaf Italian bread, sliced

Slice tomatoes into a shallow serving platter, cutting them about ½-inch thick. Slice cheese ¼-inch thick into pieces about the size of the tomato slices. Line a platter with slices of Italian bread; place tomatoes, cheese and onion over the bread. Sprinkle chopped basil, salt and pepper. Then drizzle with olive oil and vinegar. Serve immediately. *Makes 6 servings.*

Laura DeSario
St. Francis of Assisi Lodge #2629

MY DAUGHTER'S PASTA SALAD PARMESAN

¼ cup peanut oil
2 cups fresh broccoli florets
¼ cup sliced scallions
1 clove garlic, minced
½ teaspoon fresh basil leaves
½ teaspoon salt

½ pound pasta, cooked and drained (bow ties or rotelli go well with this)
½ cup freshly grated Parmesan cheese
1 cup cherry or other tomatoes, cut up in bite-size pieces

In large skillet, heat oil over medium heat. Add broccoli, scallions, garlic, basil and salt. Toss and stir until broccoli is tender-crisp, about 4 minutes. Remove from heat. Toss with pasta, cheese and tomatoes. Chill well before serving.
Serves 6.

Sybil DeSimone
Romanesque Lodge #2198

PASTA SALAD PRIMAVERA

8 ounces pasta shells (cooked and drained)
1 tablespoon extra-virgin olive oil
2 medium zucchini
½ pound fresh mushrooms, thinly sliced

1 large red pepper, cut into thin 1-inch strips
¼ pound snow peas
¾ cup Italian dressing
2 tablespoons freshly grated Romano cheese

In large bowl, toss pasta shells with oil. Cut zucchini into ¼-inch slices. Add zucchini, mushrooms, peppers and snow peas to the pasta shells.

Pour dressing over salad. Just before serving, toss the salad with grated cheese.
Serves 6 to 8.

Darlene Mazzacone
St. Francis of Assisi Lodge #2629

BREAD CRUMB TOPPING FOR VEGETABLES

2 tablespoons olive oil
⅓ cup finely chopped onion
1 clove garlic, minced

½ cup Italian style bread
   crumbs

In skillet, heat olive oil. Add onion and garlic. Cook 3 minutes or until tender. Add bread crumbs and cook 3 minutes more, stirring occasionally.

Serve over hot cooked vegetables.

Olga V. Pacil
Geneva American Italian Ladies Lodge #2397A

STUFFED MUSHROOMS

1 (3 pound) basket large
   mushrooms
1 (8 ounce) package
   Pepperidge Farms herb-
   seasoned stuffing
2 medium onions, finely
   chopped

4 stalks celery, finely chopped
¾ stick of butter or margarine
1 egg
3 tablespoons grated Romano
   cheese
2 cups water

Wash mushrooms, remove stems. Chop mushroom stems, add celery, onions and fry together in oil in a large fry pan. Parboil mushroom caps in boiling water for 10 minutes, drain and put on paper towels. Melt ¾ stick butter or margarine in a saucepan with 2 cups boiling water.

In a large bowl add package of stuffing, add stems, celery and onion mixture. Slowly add water with butter or margarine (about half), mix well. Add beaten egg and grated cheese, salt and pepper to taste. Add more water until you reach the consistency you like. Stuff mushroom caps using a teaspoon and make a well-rounded "dome". Place on a greased cookie sheet and bake at 350° for 25 minutes.
Makes about 50.

May be used with chicken, turkey, or served as an appetizer.

Evelyn Nelson
Loggia Glen Cove #1016

POTATO CROQUETTES

5 or 6 potatoes, boiled and
   mashed
2 eggs, 1 for mixture, 1 for
   dipping

½ teaspoon salt
½ teaspoon pepper

To dip:
bread crumbs (plain)
flour
3 or 4 cloves garlic, cut fine

parsley
½ cup Italian cheese

Mix into mashed potatoes, 1 egg, salt, pepper, garlic, cheese and parsley. Refrigerate mix for 1 hour or more.

Remove from refrigerator and roll into oblong form. After rolled, dip each croquette into flour, egg and bread crumbs. After dipped, leave at room temperature about ½ hour. Then fry in oil over medium heat.

Mathilda Riccardello
Daughters & Sons of Italian Heritage Lodge #2428

STUFFED ONIONS

6 large onions, cut in half and
   boiled until cooked
4 pounds spinach, cook,
   squeeze out water, chop
   fine
1 pound chopped meat,
   sautéed with garlic
6 eggs, beaten lightly

¼ pound grated Parmesan
   cheese
salt and pepper to taste
¼ cup parsley, chopped fine
1 cup bread crumbs,
   unseasoned
6 cloves of garlic, chopped fine
   and mixed with meat

Mixture must be like the consistency of yogurt. You can get this mixture by using more or less bread crumbs.

Get cooked onion halves ready to stuff with a mixture of all the above ingredients.

Place stuffed onions on "cookie sheet pan with edges on all 4 sides." Sprinkle onions with a little olive oil. Place pan in 400° to 425° pre-heated oven for 40 minutes. Turn onions over in 20 minutes. Onions have to start turning brownish.

George and Ann Dormani
Cellini Lodge #2206

CARROTS WITH GARLIC AND BASIL

1 pound carrots, sliced
¼ cup minced basil
1 teaspoon lemon juice

1-2 cloves garlic, minced
black pepper to taste

Place carrots in a glass pie plate with 2 tablespoons water. Cover with vented plastic wrap; microwave on high power for about 3 minutes.

Coat a large frying pan with nonstick spray. Sauté carrots, garlic, basil and lemon juice until fragrant, about 3 minutes. Sprinkle with pepper. *Serves 4.*

Jeanne P. Abbadessa
Cellini Lodge #2206

JETTA'S POTATO PATTIES

4 cups instant potatoes
5 cups bread crumbs
¼ cup grated cheese
1 tablespoon parsley

¼ teaspoon oregano
¼ teaspoon basil
3 extra-large eggs

Put enough oil in skillet to fry patties; if you use a nonstick skillet, much less oil is needed.

Mix together: crumbs, cheese, parsley, oregano, basil and eggs with the mashed potatoes that you have prepared according to the directions on the box. (Can omit salt and butter if on a salt-free diet.) When all ingredients are thoroughly mixed together, form patties and fry in large skillet on medium heat, until golden brown. Drain on paper towels.
Recipe makes about 45 patties.

Can be made the day before; or in advance of serving and reheated in the microwave.

Concetta (Jetta) Curreri
Italian American Women's Lodge #1979

ITALIAN GREEN BEANS WITH HERBS

1 pound Italian green beans
½ teaspoon salt
1 tablespoon olive oil
4 shallots, peeled
2 tablespoons minced fresh
    basil

½ teaspoon crumbled dried
    oregano
2 tablespoons lemon juice
3 tablespoons chopped fresh
    Italian parsley

Wash beans, remove top and tail. Cut diagonally into 1½-inch pieces. Put in a large saucepan, cover with cold water, add salt and bring to a boil. Blanch beans for 5 to 8 minutes, until barely tender but still crunchy. Drain and rinse with cold water. Drain again.

Heat oil in skillet, add minced shallots and sauté until they are translucent. Add basil and oregano, stir for 1 minute. Then turn beans into skillet and sauté, turning them until all beans are coated with oil and herbs. Pour lemon juice, add parsley and serve hot.
Serves 4 to 6.

Lucy F. Codella
Aquileia Ladies Lodge #935

BAKED CANNELLINI BEANS

½ cup chopped onion
1 clove garlic, minced
1 tablespoon cooking oil
2 (20 ounce) cans cannellini
    beans, drained
½ teaspoon oregano

1 (16 ounce) can tomato sauce
4 ounces pepperoni, chopped
½ teaspoon basil
1 cup shredded provolone
    cheese (4 ounces)
dash pepper

Cook onion and garlic in oil until tender. Stir in beans, tomato sauce, pepperoni and seasonings. Bake in 2-quart casserole uncovered at 350° for 50 minutes. Sprinkle with cheese, bake 5 more minutes until cheese is melted.

Carol Piccirillo
Gabriele D'Annunzio Lodge #321

BAKED ZUCCHINI

2 tablespoons butter or
   margarine
1 small onion, minced
6 small zucchini, sliced thin
salt and pepper to taste
1 tablespoon parsley

½ cup seasoned bread crumbs
¼ cup grated cheese (Romano
   or Parmesan)
¼ cup shredded mozzarella
   cheese

In a skillet, melt butter and sauté onion until tender. Add remaining ingredients. Spread into a greased 10-inch pie plate or other suitable baking dish. Bake for 25 minutes in a 400° oven.
Serves 4 to 6.

Dorothea Yarcel
Aida Ladies Lodge #2163A

ZUCCHINI BOATS I

8 small size zucchini
1 small onion, cut up
½-1 cup sliced mushrooms
4-6 ounces tomato sauce

salt, pepper, garlic powder or
   minced garlic, parsley or
   parsley flakes, to taste
mozzarella cheese
2 tablespoons olive oil (for
   sauté)

Trim ends and cut zucchini lengthwise. With a teaspoon, scoop out the pulp until a shell of approximately ⅛-inch remains (handle carefully). Place shells in steamer basket for approximately 5 minutes (do not overcook). Remove and cool slightly.

Mix pulp, onion, mushrooms, and seasonings; sauté gently over medium heat, stirring often for approximately 5 minutes. Add tomato sauce and blend with mixture (do not make soupy). Remove from heat and fill shells. Top with shredded mozzarella cheese and bake 20 minutes, or until mixture is bubbly and cheese is melted.

Theresa Romeo
Ann Bambino Lodge #2353

ZUCCHINI BOATS II

3 medium zucchini, washed
   and trimmed
3 tablespoons butter or
   margarine
2 tablespoons chopped onion
27 saltine crackers, unsalted
   tops, finely rolled (about 1
   cup of crumbs)

1 medium tomato, seeded and
   diced (about ¾ cup)
½ teaspoon salt
½ teaspoon basil leaves
dash ground black pepper
3 ounces Swiss or Cheddar
   cheese, grated (about ¾ cup)
parsley sprigs, optional

Cook zucchini in boiling water 10 to 15 minutes or until just tender; cool. Cut in half lengthwise. Leaving a ¼-inch border around the edges, carefully scoop out center, chop. Heat butter or margarine, sauté onion until golden. Combine with chopped zucchini, crumbs, and the next four ingredients; spoon into zucchini shells. Place in a shallow baking dish; top with cheese. Bake in preheated moderate oven (350°) for 15 minutes.
Makes 6 (about 5 ounce) servings.

Jennie C. Tompkins
Aquileia Ladies Lodge #935

ZUCCHINI PATTIES

2 medium-sized zucchini,
   shredded with skins
4 eggs, beaten
1 teaspoon chopped garlic

1 tablespoon chopped parsley
1 tablespoon crushed mint
1 cup grated Parmesan cheese
bread crumbs

Mix all of the above ingredients adding enough bread crumbs to hold mixture together. Drop by teaspoon or by tablespoon, depending upon which size you prefer, into hot olive oil until cooked. Drain on paper towel and serve.

Can be frozen and reheated.

Jean Giambra
Vincent Lombardi Lodge #2270

ZUCCHINI PARMESAN

1 large or 2 small zucchini
1½ cups or 1 (16 ounce) can/jar
   tomato sauce
8 slices domestic provolone
   cheese
6 ounces Parmesan cheese

2-3 teaspoons garlic powder or
   2 large cloves of garlic
1 teaspoon olive oil
salt, pepper and oregano to
   taste

Wash and slice zucchini crosswise (leave skin and seeds intact). Quick fry (approximately 10 seconds) on each side of slice. Remove from pan and place on paper towels or brown bag to absorb oil.

In baking dish (glass is best), put 1 to 2 spoonfuls of sauce to coat bottom. Sprinkle with Parmesan. Layer in 3 slices of provolone, sprinkle with garlic. Layer in zucchini. Sprinkle with garlic, Parmesan, salt, pepper and oregano to taste. Layer in a few spoonfuls of sauce. Layer in remaining provolone. Sprinkle with garlic and then sprinkle heavy layer of Parmesan. Cover gently with remaining sauce. Sprinkle again with Parmesan.

Bake at 300° to 350° for 20 minutes. (Electric oven use 300°, gas oven use 350°, microwave at medium heat for 9 minutes).
Yield: 4 to 6 servings.

Note: You can substitute mozzarella or scamorza cheese for provolone.

Grace Ruggiero-Ziegler
St. Francis of Assisi Lodge #2629

"DOLLY'S" STUFFED ITALIAN PEPPERS

10 Italian frying peppers
½ cup grated Parmesan cheese
1 tablespoon black pepper
1 teaspoon salt
2 cloves minced garlic

2 tablespoons chopped fresh
  parsley
2 loaves of day-old Italian
  bread
olive oil

Remove crust and soak day-old Italian bread in a small amount of warm water for a few minutes. Squeeze out as much water as you can from the bread. Place moist bread in a medium-size bowl and combine with cheese, salt, pepper, garlic and parsley. Remove stem and seeds from Italian peppers. Wash and dry thoroughly. Loosely stuff peppers with bread stuffing. Coat bottom of a baking pan with oil, turn peppers in oil so all of the pepper is slightly coated with oil and bake at 400° for approximately ½ hour or until peppers are cooked.

Nancy Quinn
Per Sempre Ladies Lodge #2344A

STUFFED PEPPERS

Pepperoni Imbotitti

¾ cup toasted bread crumbs
¼ pound soppressata, cut into
   tiny pieces
¼ cup grated caciocavallo
   cheese
¼ pound fresh diced
   mozzarella cheese

¼ cup golden raisins, soaked
¾ cup pine nuts
salt and pepper to taste
4-6 green bell peppers
4 tablespoons olive oil
2 cups smooth tomato sauce

Mix the bread crumbs, soppressata, caciocavallo, mozzarella, raisins and pine nuts. Salt and pepper to taste.

Cut a ring around the top of the peppers. Pull out lid and remove all seeds. Stuff peppers loosely with the bread crumbs and soppressata mixture. Put top back on.

Preheat oven to 350°. Pour 1 tablespoon olive oil over each pepper and stand side by side in baking pan. Cover with tomato sauce and bake 50 minutes, adding water if necessary to prevent burning. Transfer the peppers to a platter. Serve warm.
Serves 4 to 6.

Sam DiTrapani
Per Sempre Lodge #2344

STUFFED EGGPLANT
(A la Rex)

4 small eggplants
2 cups onions, chopped
½ cup olive oil
8 plum tomatoes (peeled and
chopped)
1 egg
½ cup grated locatelli cheese
¼ pound fresh mozzarella
(chopped)

¼ cup Italian parsley
(chopped)
2 tablespoons capers (chopped)
1½ dozen green olives (pitted)
2 cups marinara sauce
½ cup dry unseasoned bread
crumbs
2 tablespoons olive oil

Cut eggplant in half lengthwise and hollow them out. Do not puncture skin. Chop pulp of eggplant into small pieces.

Sauté onions in oil until lightly golden. Add eggplant. Sauté about 3 minutes over medium heat. Add tomatoes and stir. Cool.

Combine eggplant mixture with egg, cheeses, parsley, capers and olives. Stuff eggplant shells with mixture. Sprinkle with bread crumbs and 2 tablespoons of olive oil. Bake in preheated 425° oven for 20 minutes, until a crust forms on top. Serve at room temperature.
Yield: 8 servings.

Victor Parise
Columbus Lodge #2143

STUFFED EGGPLANT

1 large eggplant
2 eggs
1 pound ground meat

1 cup bread crumbs
salt and pepper to taste

Cut eggplant lengthwise. Scoop out pulp leaving ½-inch wall and boil pulp for 5 minutes. Drain and add egg, ground meat, bread crumbs, salt and pepper. Refill eggplant halves with mixture and sprinkle with grated cheese on top and bake at 350° for almost 1 hour. Add spaghetti sauce 15 minutes before serving, if desired.

Angela Parise
Vincent Lombardi Lodge #2270

FRITTELE DE ZUCCHINI

Zucchini Fritters

1 pound small zucchini, well
   scrubbed in cold water
3 tablespoons chopped parsley
1 teaspoon chopped garlic
½ cup grated Parmesan cheese
3 eggs (not too large)

¼ cup fine, dry unflavored
   bread crumbs, plus 1 cup
   spread on a plate
salt and pepper to taste
vegetable oil

Using grater or food processor, shred zucchini using large shredding holes. Put zucchini in a bowl with parsley, garlic and grated cheese.

Beat eggs and add to zucchini. Add ¼ cup bread crumbs, a few grindings of black pepper and mix.

In a skillet put enough oil to fry fritters, about ½ inch deep. Turn heat to medium high. When oil is hot, add some salt to zucchini, mix quickly and form patties about 3 inches in diameter and ½-inch thick. Dredge patties in bread crumbs on the plate. Fry in oil. Turn when they are golden on one side. Put on a plate lined with paper towels to drain. Serve hot.

Note: Do not salt until you are ready to fry or they will throw off too much liquid.

Lucy Fiscina
Daughters and Sons of Italian Heritage Lodge #2428

BAKED BROCCOLI STEMS

2 cups ricotta cheese
2 cups broccoli stems,
   cooked/chopped
½ cup grated Parmesan cheese

¼ cup flour
2 eggs, slightly beaten
salt and pepper to taste

Combine ricotta cheese, broccoli, half amount of Parmesan cheese, flour, eggs, salt and pepper.

Spray pyrex pie plate with nonstick vegetable spray and spoon in ingredients. Sprinkle with remaining grated cheese. Bake 30 minutes at 350° or until the top is lightly browned.
Serves 6 to 8.

Ellen Schrader
Santa Rosalia Lodge #2131

BROCCOLI RABE A LA BARESE

8 links sweet sausage with
    fennel
2 pounds broccoli rabe
1 (8 ounce) can chicken broth

6 cloves fresh garlic, minced
1 pound orecchiette pasta,
    cooked

In fry pan, sauté garlic in small amount of olive oil. Remove sausage from casing and add to garlic. Place broccoli rabe on top of cooked sausage and add chicken broth. Steam until tender. Pour over cooked orecchiette. Toss and serve. Top with grated Romano cheese.

Enjoy!

Annette Lankewish
Marcus Aurelius Lodge #2321

BROCCOLI RABE WITH SAUSAGE

3 pounds broccoli rabe (more
    or less)
1½ pounds of Italian sausage
2 cloves of garlic (whole or
    minced)

dash of hot pepper
salt to taste
1 tablespoon olive oil

Remove tough stems from broccoli, wash and leave in water until ready for them.

Heat oil in large pot, sauté sausage until brown. Add garlic and seasoning.

Remove broccoli from water leaving some water on them and add to the sausage. Cover and cook for approximately 10 minutes or until the broccoli is cooked. Serve with fresh Italian bread.
Serves 4.

Julia Acompora
Italian Heritage Lodge #2227

EGGPLANT WITH SHRIMP FILLING

1½ pounds eggplant
½ teaspoon salt
¼ teaspoon pepper
2 tablespoons butter
¼ chopped onion
2 tablespoons chopped green
    pepper

1 clove garlic, minced
2 cups shrimp
1 cup soft bread crumbs
2 tablespoons pimento,
    chopped
1 cup buttered bread crumbs

Split eggplant in half lengthwise. Cook covered in a small amount of boiling water for 10 minutes or until slightly tender. Remove from water and drain. Scoop out pulp from the center of eggplant leaving ¼-inch shell. Set shells aside.

Finely chop the pulp. Melt butter and add onions. Sauté onions until transparent. Add pulp, garlic and green pepper. Clean shrimp and chop. Add shrimp, bread crumbs, pimento, salt and pepper to the mixture. Mix thoroughly and spoon mixture into eggplant shells. Cover tops with buttered bread crumbs. Bake in a 375° oven for 20 to 30 minutes or until crumbs are browned.
Serves 8 to 10.

Judith Scandiffio
Romanesque Lodge #2198

EGGPLANT ROLLATINI

2 large eggplants, sliced
    lengthwise
2 eggs, beaten
bread crumbs
garlic, finely chopped

ricotta cheese
mozzarella cheese, grated
parsley, chopped
marinara sauce

Dip eggplant slices in eggs, then in bread crumbs seasoned with garlic. Brown lightly; lay on a platter. Mix ricotta, mozzarella, and parsley. Spoon a heaping tablespoon onto each eggplant slice and roll, secure with a toothpick or lay seam side down. Lay in broiling pan and cover with marinara sauce. Bake at 450° for 10 to 15 minutes.

Donna Petrucci
Donne D'Italia Lodge #2330

ESCAROLE WITH BLACK OLIVES

2 medium heads escarole
½ can anchovies
½ can pitted black olives

4 cloves garlic (sliced)
3 tablespoons olive oil
salt and pepper to taste

Wash escarole thoroughly and drain.

In large frying pan, brown 2 cloves of garlic in oil. Place half of escarole in pan. Cover and simmer for 10 minutes. Place anchovies, olives and remaining garlic in a layer over escarole. Add salt and pepper to taste. Add remaining escarole on top. Cover and simmer 1 hour.

If juices evaporate before escarole is completely cooked, add a little water to prevent sticking and burning.
Yield: 2 servings.

Gina Marie Cangemi-Coffen
Donatello Lodge #2559

STUFFED ARTICHOKES

4 medium-size artichokes
1 cup bread crumbs
5 tablespoons grated cheese
2 cloves garlic, chopped

2 tablespoons parsley, chopped
6 tablespoons olive oil
salt and pepper to taste

Cut off stems near to artichoke base and about ½-inch of tips. Remove tough outer leaves. Wash carefully, so as not to have fall apart. Tap on table gently, to spread leaves open. Shake out all water.

Mix thoroughly bread crumbs, grated cheese, chopped parsley, garlic, salt and pepper. Divide mixture into 4 parts; distribute one portion between the leaves of each artichoke. Then close.

Place upright in saucepan to fit snugly. Pour 1 tablespoon of olive oil over each artichoke. Put remaining oil in saucepan and add 1 cup of water. Cover tightly; cook slowly for 1 hour or until tender. Watch water, if it evaporates add a little more. Test by pulling out leaf. If it comes out easily, artichokes are done.
Serves 4.

Lucy Codella
Aquileia Ladies Lodge #935

ARTICHOKES & MUSHROOMS

2 boxes fresh mushrooms
1 (16 ounce) can artichoke
  hearts
diced garlic

seasoned bread crumbs
grating cheese
olive oil

Wash and slice mushrooms. Drain artichokes and cut into quarters. Coat roasting pan with oil. In large bowl mix together mushrooms, artichokes and diced garlic. Add mixture to pan lightly covering bottom of pan. Generously sprinkle bread crumbs and cheese over vegetables. Add more mixture and again cover well with cheese and bread crumbs.

Drizzle olive oil all over top of mixture, especially all around the sides of the pan. Add enough oil to moisten, taking care not to saturate.

Cover with aluminum foil and bake at 350° for 30 minutes. Uncover and continue to bake another 20 minutes until lightly browned.

Godere!

Betty Galioto
Dr. Vincenzo Sellaro Lodge #2319

DOLCE

DESSERTS

NEW YORK OSIA FILIAL LODGES

•**Donne D'Italia Lodge #2330**, West Islip, Charter issued 1975: This lodge was initiated on Palm Sunday, March 23, 1975 by a famous Degree Team from Winchester, Massachusetts. It was the first women's lodge to be formed in Suffolk County.

•**Per Sempre Lodge #2344**, Rosedale, Charter issued 1975: This lodge located in southeast Queens, holds the distinction of being the largest men's lodge in the City of New York. The name "Per Sempre" was chosen with the hope that this lodge will remain "forever".

•**Per Sempre Ladies Lodge #2344A**, Rosedale, Charter issued 1977. This women's lodge is the "Sister" lodge to the Per Sempre Lodge and holds the distinction of being the largest ladies lodge in the City of New York.

•**Ann Bambino Lodge #2353**, Massapequa Park, Charter issued 1976: Named after Ann Bambino, a community activist, who died at an early age.

•**Pope John XXIII Lodge #2360**, The Bronx, Charter issued 1976: Pope John XXIII brought about great changes, through the second Vatican Council during his brief reign (1958-1963).

•**Italo Balbo Lodge #2361**, Uniondale, Charter issued 1976: The lodge was named after the famous aviator who flew an expedition of several planes from Orbetello, Italy, to the United States in July 1933. This flight demonstrated the feasibility of transatlantic air service.

•**Auburn Lodge #2368**, Auburn, Charter issued 1976: Named after the city of Auburn on the northern shore of beautiful Owasco Lake, the second of the five finger lakes.

•**Giovanni Caboto Lodge #2372**, Bellmore, Charter issued 1976: Giovanni Caboto (John Cabot) was born in Genoa in 1451. He was a famous explorer who planted the first English flag on American soil establishing England's claim to most of North America.

•**American Venice Lodge #2384**, Copiague, Charter issued 1977: Named after a section of the south shore of western Long Island in Suffolk County that had many canals and resembled Venice.

•**Leonardo Da Vinci Lodge #2385**, Inwood, Charter issued 1977: Leonardo Da Vinci was an Italian artist, the supreme example of Renaissance genius. His greatest works include the painting "Mona Lisa" and his fresco "The Last Supper". Da Vinci was also a great inventor and scientist who drew up plans that anticipated such inventions as the helicopter, submarine, machine gun and the automobile.

•**Santa Maria Lodge #2387**, The Bronx, Charter issued 1977: This lodge was named after the famous flagship used by Columbus when he made his first voyage of discovery to America in 1492.

•**Geneva Lodge #2397**, Geneva, Charter issued 1977: Named after the city of Geneva on the northern shores of beautiful Seneca Lake, the fourth of the five Finger Lakes.

•**Geneva American Italian Ladies Lodge #2397A** Geneva, Charter issued 1977: This Geneva women's lodge is known by its acronym, the GAIL lodge.

(Continued on next divider page)

HILLARY CLINTON'S CHOCOLATE CHIP COOKIES

1½ cups unsifted all-purpose
  flour
1 teaspoon salt
1 teaspoon baking soda
1 cup solid vegetable
  shortening
1 cup firmly packed light
  brown sugar

½ cup granulated sugar
1 teaspoon vanilla
2 eggs
2 cups old-fashioned rolled
  oats
1 (12 ounce) package semi-
  sweet chocolate chips

Preheat oven to 350°. Grease baking sheets. Combine flour, salt and baking soda. Beat together shortening, sugars and vanilla in a large bowl until creamy. Add eggs, beating until light and fluffy. Gradually beat in flour mixture and rolled oats. Stir in chocolate chips. Drop batter by well-rounded teaspoonsful on to greased baking sheets. Bake 8 to 10 minutes or until golden. Cool cookies on sheets on wire rack for 2 minutes. Remove cookies to wire rack to cool completely.

Hillary Rodham Clinton

ITALIAN FILLING FOR CAKES AND COOKIES

1 (1 pint) jar apple butter
1 (1 pint) jar grape jam
1 grated orange rind
2 tablespoons instant cocoa
small pieces of chocolate,
  chopped

1 tablespoon anise flavoring or
  liqueur
¼ cup ground nuts

Mix above ingredients all together. If too loose, add bread crumbs.

This can be refrigerated to store for 6 to 8 months.

Cecile Marra
Le Amiche Lodge #2550

ADELINA'S RAISIN CAKE

2 eggs, separated
2 heaping tablespoons Crisco
   shortening
1 cup brown sugar
1 cup white sugar
1½ teaspoons cinnamon
1½ teaspoons nutmeg
1½ teaspoons cloves

¾ teaspoon salt
1 teaspoon baking powder
2 teaspoons baking soda
4 cups sifted flour
4 cups water
2 cups raisins (boil ahead,
   reduce to 2 cups water)

In a large bowl, combine egg yolks, Crisco, sugars, cinnamon, nutmeg, cloves, salt and baking soda. Then add flour and water to mixture.

Beat egg whites until fluffy but not stiff. Add egg whites, raisins, and baking powder last. Spray cookie sheet (with side) with Pam or line with wax paper. Bake in 350° oven for 45 minutes.

Dolores Guerrera Ross
Italian American Women's Lodge #1979

AMARETTO CAKE

2 packages vanilla My-T-Fine
   pudding
2 packages chocolate My-T-
   Fine pudding
1 cup amaretto liqueur

½ pint heavy cream
2 packages Stella D'Oro
   Almond Toast
1 package slivered almonds
7 cups milk

Mix 2 packages of vanilla pudding with ½ cup of amaretto liqueur and 3½ cups of milk. Cook according to pudding directions. Allow to cool slightly. Do the same with the chocolate pudding.

Line a buttered spring pan with Almond Toast. (Fill spaces with broken cookies.) Cover with vanilla pudding. Place another layer of cookies over the vanilla pudding and cover with chocolate pudding. Refrigerate ½ hour.

Before serving, whip cream and cover cake. Add slivered almonds to decorate.

Terri DeGennaro
Italian Heritage Lodge #2227

CASSATA A LA SICILIANA

1 pound cake, 16 ounces
1 (15 ounce) carton ricotta
   cheese
2 tablespoons heavy cream
¼ cup fine granulated sugar

3 tablespoons Galliano liqueur
4 ounces semi-sweet chocolate,
   chopped coarsely
2 tablespoons chopped candied
   fruit

Frosting:
12 ounces semi-sweet
   chocolate, cut into small
   pieces
⅔ cup strong black coffee

½ pound unsalted butter, cut
   into ½-inch pieces,
   thoroughly chilled

Slice off end crusts of the pound cake and level its top. Cut cake horizontally into 4 (½-inch) lengths.

Rub ricotta through a coarse sieve into a mixing bowl. Beat until smooth, then add cream, sugar and liqueur. Fold in chopped chocolate and fruit.

Divide filling into 3 portions. On a flat serving plate, place a layer of pound cake, then spread with some of the ricotta filling. Add more layers and more ricotta filling ending with a plain slice of cake on top. Refrigerate a couple of hours to make it firm.

Make a frosting: Melt chocolate and coffee in a small, heavy saucepan over low heat, stirring until dissolved. Remove from heat, beat in butter a piece at a time, until mixture becomes smooth. Chill this mixture to spreading consistency. Frost cake, swirling the frosting into decorative designs. Chill cake again for at least a day before serving, so flavors can blend.

Yield: 8 to 10 servings.

Note: Brush layers with melted apricot jam before filling.

Terrie Vanasco
Italo Balbo Lodge #2361

ITALIAN LOVE CAKE

1 angel food cake	2 cups heavy cream
½ cup Amaretto di Saronno	1 (6 ounce) package semi-sweet
1 pint pistachio ice cream	real chocolate morsels
1 pint strawberry ice cream	

With a sharp serrated knife using a sawing motion, cut the cake into three layers. Sprinkle layers with 6 tablespoons of Amaretto di Saronno.

Place one layer on a serving platter. Cut ice cream into slices and place pistachio ice cream on bottom layer. Top with second cake layer and a layer of strawberry ice cream. Top with third cake layer. Place in freezer.

In a bowl, mix heavy cream and remaining Amaretto and beat until very thick. Frost the sides and top of the cake and replace in freezer.

Melt chocolate over very low heat until smooth. Spread chocolate in ¼-inch thick layer on foil and chill until chocolate hardens. With a small cookie cutter, cut hearts out of the chocolate and place on top of cake.

Freeze cake until ready to serve.
Makes one (9-inch) cake.

Terri Sinocchi
Le Amiche Lodge #2550

ITALIAN FRUIT CAKE

Torta Di Frutta

½ package seedless raisins
1½ cups sugar
2 cups water, boiled and
    cooled
1 package candied orange peel
1 package candied pineapple
½ cup Wesson oil
2 eggs

1 teaspoon baking powder
1 teaspoon baking soda
3 cups flour
1 package candied cherries
2 teaspoons vanilla
1 teaspoon salt
½ cup chopped walnuts

Mix raisins, sugar, water and fruit peels. Add dry ingredients and eggs one at a time and Wesson oil. Mix well together. Pour in tube pan; add half walnuts and cherries on top. Bake 1½ hours at 300°.

Sophie Sciame
Cellini Lodge #2206

ZUCCHINI CAKE

4 eggs
1 cup oil
3 cups sugar
3 cups grated raw zucchini
3 cups flour

3 teaspoons baking powder
1 teaspoon baking soda
1½ teaspoons cinnamon
½ cup nuts
½ cup raisins

Frosting:
8 ounces cream cheese
¼ pound margarine or butter

2 cups confectioners sugar
1 teaspoon vanilla

Mix eggs and oil together and beat well. Add sugar and grated zucchini.

In separate bowl, mix together flour, baking powder, baking soda, cinnamon, nuts and raisins. Add this to zucchini mixture.

Bake at 350° for 1 hour in a 9 x 13-inch pan or tube pan.

Donna Brocchi Allen
Aquileia Ladies Lodge #935

TORTA DI CIOCCOLATA E ALBUMI

8 egg whites (about 1¼ cups),
   room temperature
½ cup unsweetened cocoa
   powder
1 cup sugar
3 tablespoons corn oil

⅓ cup hazelnuts, lightly
   toasted and coarsely
   chopped
⅓ cup finely chopped walnut
   meats

Beat 6 egg whites until dry and set aside.

Combine the cocoa with the sugar, oil, and remaining unbeaten egg whites in a large bowl. Add the nuts and mix well Add one quarter of the beaten egg whites and mix again. Fold in the remaining beaten egg whites and pour into an oiled and lightly floured 9-inch cake pan.

Bake in a preheated 350° oven for about 30 minutes, or until a toothpick inserted in the center comes out dry. Transfer to a wire rack to cool, then invert the torta over a cake dish and sprinkle with confectioners sugar.
Yield: 8 servings.

Cake does not rise very high (like a one layer cake). It has an intense chocolate flavor but still delicate. There is no flour. Cake batter should be prepared quickly and baked at the same time. Let cool thoroughly.

Anne Klein
Arturo Toscanini Lodge #2107

ITALIAN CHEESE CAKE I

3 pounds ricotta cheese
12 large eggs
1 bottle orange extract
1 bottle lemon extract

1½ cups sugar
1 small heavy cream
dash of anise extract to taste

Mix ricotta cheese, eggs, sugar, heavy cream and extracts all together with hand mixer in large bowl. Pour into spring pan.

Bake in preheated 350° oven for 1 hour. Turn oven off and let stand in oven 1 hour or until top browns. Refrigerate.

Serve plain or dust with confectioners sugar.

Barbara Lupo
Andrea Doria Lodge #2201

ITALIAN CHEESE CAKE II

4½ pounds ricotta cheese
10 eggs
2 cups sugar
4 tablespoons chopped citron

6 graham crackers, finely
ground
pinch of salt
2 teaspoons vanilla
2 tablespoons lemon rind

Mix ricotta cheese, sugar and salt. Add 1 egg at a time, mixing well. Add vanilla, lemon rind and citron.

Lightly grease spring pan with margarine. Dust lightly with graham crackers. Fill and bake at 350° for about 1 hour. Top should be slightly browned. Let cool before removing from pan.

Jean Rivieccio
Per Sempre Ladies Lodge #2344A

RICOTTA CAKE

2 pounds ricotta cheese
4 eggs
¾ cup sugar
2 teaspoons vanilla
1 package Duncan Hines
    yellow cake mix

1 box instant lemon pudding
3 eggs
⅓ cup oil
1 cup water

Beat first 4 ingredients until smooth. Set aside.

Prepare cake mix with pudding, eggs, water and oil. Mix together until smooth and pour into 10 x 13-inch pan. Drizzle ricotta mixture over cake batter.

Bake in 350° oven for 1 hour. (Cake is done when tester is slightly moist.)

After cake is cooled, dust with confectioners sugar.

Stella Grillo
Marcus Aurelius Lodge #2321

RICOTTA PIE I

4 ounces cream cheese, softened
½ cup light brown sugar
3 egg yolks
1 pound ricotta cheese
1 teaspoon vanilla
3 egg whites

8 ounces plus 8 ounces heavy cream plus 1 tablespoon powdered sugar
6 ounces semi-sweet chocolate bits
1 pre-cooked (9-inch) pie shell

Beat cream cheese and sugar together; add egg yolks and beat. Add ricotta cheese, melt chocolate bits and add slowly to mixture. Beat egg whites stiff and gently fold into mixture with vanilla.

Beat 8 ounces heavy cream and add to mixture slowly. Pour mixture into pie shell and refrigerate several hours till set.

Beat 8 ounces heavy cream and sugar and spread over pie.

Frances Barbera
Romanesque Lodge #2198

RICOTTA PIE II

1 pound ricotta cheese (one 15 ounce container will do)
⅛ teaspoon salt (optional)
4 eggs
1 cup sugar

¼ cup flour
1 tablespoon vanilla
grated orange peel (no white part)

Beat eggs until foamy. Gradually add sugar while still beating eggs until mixture is thick and piled softly. Mix other ingredients and blend into egg mixture until smooth.

Pour into 9-inch square pyrex dish. Bake at 350° in middle of oven until firm and lightly golden brown for about 50 to 60 minutes. Remove from oven and place on cooling rack. Refrigerate when cooled. Sprinkle with confectioners sugar before serving.
Serves 8 to 10.

Dorothea Yarcel
Aida Ladies Lodge #2163A

RICOTTA PIE III

½ cup graham cracker crumbs
¼ cup margarine, softened
½ teaspoon cinnamon
1½ teaspoons unflavored
    gelatin
½ cup 1% fat-free milk

½ cup semi-sweet chocolate
    pieces
½ cup blanched almonds
1 pound ricotta cheese
½ teaspoon almond extract

Combine cracker crumbs, margarine and cinnamon. Mix well. Press crumbs into a 9-inch pie plate. Bake crust in oven at 350° for 8 minutes. Cool.

Sprinkle gelatin over milk. Let stand for 5 minutes to soften. Heat over hot water until gelatin is dissolved. Cool. Chill until thick as unbeaten egg whites.

Put chocolate pieces and almonds in blender. Whirl for 1 minute. Add ricotta cheese and extract. Whirl for 1 minute longer. Spoon into large bowl.

Beat gelatin mixture with electric mixer until fluffy. Fold into ricotta mixture. Spoon into cooled shell. Refrigerate 2 hours until set. Garnish with chocolate or almonds.
Serves 16.

Ramona Constantine
Geneva American Italian Ladies Lodge #2397A

PIZZA DOLCE

15 eggs, beaten very well for
    about 15 minutes
2 cups granulated sugar
¾ ounce vanilla extract

¾ ounce orange extract
1 ounce anise extract
3 pounds ricotta cheese, well
    drained

Beat together all ingredients except ricotta cheese for about 20 minutes. Add ricotta and continue beating for another 20 minutes.

Grease a medium-size baking pan and add mixture. Bake in a 350° oven for 1 hour and 20 minutes until golden brown on top.

Let cool and serve at either room temperature or from refrigerator.
Serves 8 to 10.

Mae Butera
Guglielmo Marconi Lodge #2232

ITALIAN RICE PIE

½ cup rice, cooked and drained
8 eggs, beaten until a light
   color
2 pounds ricotta cheese
2 cups sugar

grated rind of 1 orange
   and 1 lemon
juice of ½ lemon
¼ teaspoon cinnamon
1 teaspoon vanilla extract

Mix all the above ingredients together adding vanilla last. Place in a 10- or 12-inch pie crust (plain or graham cracker). Bake at 350° for about 1 hour.

Laura Cheresnik
Italian Heritage Lodge #2227

RISO AMMANTICATU

1 cup short grain rice
3 cups milk
1½ cups sugar
1 tablespoon butter
1 tablespoon unsweetened
   cocoa

⅓ cup chopped candied fruit
2 cups almonds, toasted and
   finely chopped
pinch of cinnamon
1 lemon peel (grated)

Combine the rice, milk, sugar and butter in pot. Bring mixture to a boil. Cover and let simmer for 25 minutes. Remove from heat when all the liquid has been absorbed and the rice is fluffy. Let cool.

Stir in cocoa, half the candied fruit and almonds and all of the cinnamon and lemon peel. Mix thoroughly. Spoon the rice into individual serving dishes. Decorate with the remaining almonds and candied fruit. Serve cold.
Serves 6.

Bella Cosa e Pranso.

Sam DiTrapani
Per Sempre Lodge #2344

POPATELLI

4 cups flour
2 teaspoons cinnamon
½ cup cocoa
2 teaspoons cloves
1 teaspoon baking powder

1 cup sugar
½ cup chopped nuts
½ cup raisins
⅔ cup melted shortening
1½ cups hot coffee

Mix flour, cinnamon, cocoa, cloves, baking powder and sugar. Then add remaining ingredients.

Form into balls. Bake at 350° for 8 to 10 minutes. Roll in powdered sugar or make a light frosting.

Carmela Persico
Gabriele D'Annunzio Lodge #321

CANDY COATED ALMONDS

(Torrone) (Cumbata)

10 ounces skinned almonds
½ cup sugar

1 teaspoon vanilla
1 teaspoon rum

Thoroughly coat almonds in a bowl with above ingredients. Heat enough olive oil in frying pan to cover bottom of pan on a high flame.

Stir in almonds turning constantly until they start turning a light brown and start popping. Lower flame to medium or slightly lower and continue to stir until sugar dissolves and nuts are evenly browned.

Have counter top cleaned and heavily coated with water. Use a large tablespoon or serving spoon and spoon out nuts in clusters on watered counter top.

Immediately sprinkle with confetti while still hot so they stick. Later, while still warm, loosen with spatula to prevent sticking to surface. When cooled blot bottom with paper towel and break large clusters into smaller serving pieces.

Pauline Nocella
Italo Balbo Lodge #2361

CASSATEDDI SICILIANI

2 pounds flour
½ pound Crisco (melted)
2 eggs

½ teaspoon baking powder
2 tablespoons sugar
1 cup white wine

Mix all ingredients and knead. Set aside.

Filling:
3 pounds ricotta cheese
sugar

vanilla or cinnamon
chocolate chips

Mix together. Roll out dough a small piece at a time to ¼-inch thick. Cut into circles using a glass 3 inches in diameter. Drop 1 tablespoon of filling on one side of circle. Wipe edge of circle with egg white, fold over and press. With a pin, make a few holes in top to release air. After all have been filled, deep fry in vegetable oil. Drain and sprinkle with sugar.

Veronica Martino
William C. LaMorte Lodge #2251

MAMA'S SFINGI

1¼ pounds Presto flour
   (5 cups)
3 pounds ricotta cheese
8 teaspoons sugar
6 eggs

pinch of salt
pinch of cinnamon
1 tablespoon vanilla
Mazola oil for frying

Beat ricotta and eggs together. Add sugar, cinnamon and salt. Then add sifted flour and work with hands. When oil is hot, drop teaspoon-ful of dough into oil. Sprinkle with powdered sugar when cool.

Connie Genaro
Guy Lombardo Lodge #2417

ZEPPOLE I

(Italian Fritters)

2¾ cups warm water (110° to
   115°)
1 package dry active yeast
1 tablespoon olive oil
5¼ cups unbleached flour

2 tablespoons sugar
1½ teaspoons salt
8 cups vegetable oil for frying
confectioners sugar

Place ½ cup warm water in a bowl and add yeast. Stir to dissolve and let proof for 10 minutes. Add the remaining warm water and the olive oil. Set aside.

Spoon flour into a bowl. Add sugar and salt and blend. Add flour mixture to the yeast and water and beat with a wooden spoon. It should be a loose batter but not runny. Cover with plastic wrap and let rise until doubled, about 1 hour, in a warm place.

Heat vegetable oil to 375° in a deep fryer. Using 2 soup spoons, drop rounds of batter into hot oil and fry until golden. Drain on paper towels and sprinkle on confectioners sugar.

Variation: Heat 2 cups honey in saucepan with a bit of lemon juice and drizzle over fritters. Serve warm.

Another variation: You can add ¾ cup seedless golden raisins to the batter, cover with plastic wrap and let rise.

Lucy Fiscina
Daughters and Sons of Italian Heritage Lodge #2428

ZEPPOLE II

1 large yeast cake
5 cups flour

½ teaspoon salt
2 cups warm water

Melt yeast cake in warm water. Add flour and mix well with wooden spoon. Cover and let rise for ½ hour. Add salt. Mix again and let rise until batter doubles in size. Batter will be soft and sticky.

Drop by tablespoons in hot melted fat (2 cups or more). Brown and drain zeppole. Cool. Dust with confectioners sugar.

Variation: Add anchovies and omit the confectioners sugar.

Jeanette Lodato
Giosue Carducci Lodge #226A

ZEPPOLE III

(Quick and Easy)

15 ounces ricotta cheese
15 ounces Presto flour (use
  only Presto)

2 eggs
confectioners sugar

Mix ingredients together, drop by teaspoon into hot oil and fry until brown. Remove and drain on brown paper. Roll in confectioners sugar.

Nardina Trotta
Dr. Vincenzo Sellaro Lodge #2319

QUANTI

2 cups flour
2 tablespoons sugar
2 ounces butter

grated lemon rind
2 whole eggs
6 egg yolks

Mix above ingredients in order given. Roll out in a sheet ⅛-inch thick. Cut sheet into 1 x 4 inches and twist (bow shape). Fry in deep vegetable oil. Drain on paper towel and sprinkle with powdered sugar.

Carmela Persico
Gabriele D'Annunzio Lodge #321

CANNOLI

Shells:

2 cups flour
2 tablespoons shortening
1 teaspoon sugar
½ teaspoon salt

½ cup red wine
½ cup vegetable oil
3 to 4 metal tubes, 7 inches
long x 1½ inch diameter

Combine flour, shortening, sugar and salt, wetting gradually with wine. Knead until a hard dough is formed. Cover with cloth about 1 hour. Cut dough in half and roll in thin sheet ¼-inch thick. Cut into 4 squares. Place tube diagonally across sheet. Wrap dough around tube overlapping the 2 points and seal. Heat oil. Fry 1 to 2 at a time until golden brown; cool and remove tubes. Repeat.

Filling:

3 cups ricotta cheese
½ cup confectioners sugar
½ teaspoon cinnamon (liquid)
½ tablespoon cocoa (optional)

½ teaspoon vanilla
3 tablespoons citron or candied
    orange peel

Mix ricotta with sugar. Add vanilla and fruit. Chill. Fill shells when ready to serve.
Makes 10 to 12 shells.

Vera Galante
Cellini Lodge #2206

ZUPPA INGLESE

(English Soup)

4 egg yolks
1¼ cups sugar
1 teaspoon vanilla
½ teaspoon finely shredded
  lemon peel
4 egg whites
½ teaspoon cream of tartar

1 cup flour
¼ teaspoon salt
¼ cup rum
¼ cup peach, apricot or cherry
  brandy
1 cup whipped cream
shaved chocolate

Cream filling:
½ cup sugar
1 tablespoon cornstarch
¼ teaspoon salt

1½ cups milk
4 eggs
1 teaspoon vanilla

To prepare the cake, in a small mixer bowl beat egg yolks until thick and lemon colored, about 5 minutes. Gradually add sugar, vanilla and lemon peel.

In large mixer bowl beat egg whites and cream of tartar till very stiff peaks form. Fold egg yolk mixture into egg whites. Mix flour and salt together and sift flour mixture ¼ at a time over egg mixture and fold in thoroughly. Spread batter on two greased and floured 8-inch cake pans. Bake at 350° for 20 minutes or until cake tests done. Invert pans on wire racks and cool completely before removing cake from pans.

Mix rum and brandy together in bowl.

To prepare cream filling, combine sugar, cornstarch and salt in a saucepan. Gradually stir in milk. Cook and stir until thickened and bubbly. Cook and stir 2 minutes more. Gradually stir about 1 cup of the hot mixture into eggs, slightly beaten. Then return all to hot mixture. Cook and stir until mixture thickens. Remove from heat and stir in vanilla. Place clear plastic wrap over surface of custard. Cool at room temperature.
Makes 2 cups of filling.

To assemble cake, split each cake layer horizontally. Place one slice cut side up on serving plate and sprinkle with 2 tablespoons of rum mixture. Then spread ⅓ cup cream filling over cake. Repeat same steps

(Continued on next page)

(Zuppa Inglese, continued)

2 more times and top with final cake slice and 2 last tablespoons of rum mixture.

Chill cake 5 or 6 hours.

Just before serving, whip cream and frost top and sides of cake. Garnish with chocolate.
Makes 12 servings.

Mary Teresa Purtell
Giosue Carducci Lodge #226A

CRUSTADA

3 eggs
1½ sticks margarine or butter, melted
1 jar peach preserves (or any flavor preserves)
½ cup sugar

1 teaspoon vanilla extract
1 teaspoon orange extract or grated orange skin
1 tablespoon baking powder
4 cups flour

In a large bowl, beat eggs and add sugar, continue to beat. Add melted margarine and all the above ingredients, mix well. Dough should be soft and moist but not sticking to your hands. Knead dough for about 4 or 5 minutes. Separate into 2 equal parts.

Grease a large pizza pan. Spread 1 part of the dough in pan. Flatten it evenly. Add preserves. Spread evenly. With the remaining dough, roll strips the length of the pan, covering entire top about 1½ inches apart. Criss-cross with additional strips. Where strips are crossed, press down with flat end of rounded utensil. Cook 20 to 25 minutes in 350° oven or until golden brown.

Gloria Colatosti
Arturo Toscanini Lodge #2107

TIRAMISU I

(Pick Me Up)

2 packages Italian lady fingers
3 eggs, separated
1 container mascarpone cheese
6 teaspoons sugar

1 ounce S. Marzano liqueur
6 to 7 cups black coffee (cold)
cocoa powder

Beat egg yolks with sugar until creamy. Beat egg whites in separate bowl. Add mascarpone to egg yolks and mix well. Fold in egg whites.

Dip lady fingers in coffee and layer in pan. Layer cream over lady fingers. Sift cocoa over cream. Sprinkle ⅓ liqueur over top. Repeat for 3 layers and refrigerate overnight.

Harriet Sturiano
Per Sempre Ladies Lodge #2344A

TIRAMISU II

(Pick Me Up)

4 packages lady fingers
1 round mascarpone cheese
   (approximately 1 pound)

4 egg yolks
1 cup sugar
1 tablespoon lemon extract

Mix the above by hand until blended. Then fold in 4 egg whites which have been beaten until stiff.

In a separate bowl mix the following:

6 demitasse cups of espresso
sugar to taste
2 tablespoons Strega liqueur

2 tablespoons brandy
2 tablespoons Anisette liqueur

Dip lady fingers in the coffee mixture and line the serving dish. Spread with creme mixture. Keep alternating layers of cookies and creme. Be sure to end with a top layer of creme. Decorate with candied cherry, coffee beans or chocolate chips. Refrigerate for at least 3 hours. (The longer you refrigerate, the better.)
Serves 8.

Marie Pippo
Italian Heritage Lodge #2227

ZABAGLIONE DIANA

6 egg yolks
½ cup sugar

1 cup Marsala wine

Beat egg yolks and sugar until thick. Blend in wine. Pour into top of a double boiler, stirring constantly until thick. Cool. Serve in sherbet glasses with lady fingers.

This delicious Italian dessert will enhance any special dinner.

Dolores Altomare
Romanesque Lodge #2198

PEACHES AND RASPBERRIES IN MARSALA AND WHITE WINE

4 large peaches, peeled and
halved
1 pint raspberries
2 tablespoons sugar plus more
to taste

3 tablespoons Marsala wine
approximately 3 cups dry
white wine

Spumante can be substituted for Marsala and white wine. To peel the peaches, blanch them in boiling water for 30 seconds. (Their skins should slip right off.)

Place peaches and raspberries in a large non-reactive bowl. Add 2 tablespoons sugar and toss lightly. Depending upon the sweetness of the fruit, adjust the amount of sugar as necessary. Spoon fruit mixture into a 2-quart wide mouth jar. Add Marsala and enough white wine to cover the fruits. Cap the jar of fruit and chill for 4 hours. This can be refrigerated overnight.
Makes 2 quarts.

Chris Parillo
Gabriele D'Annunzio Lodge #321

ITALIAN FRUIT SALAD

1 can crushed pineapple
1 can mandarin oranges
1 (28 ounce) can fruit cocktail
1 cup sugar
2 tablespoons flour

2 eggs, slightly beaten
dash salt
1 cup Acine de Pepe pastina
1 (9 ounce) container Cool
  Whip

Drain pineapple and oranges, saving their juices. Cook pineapple and orange juice with sugar, flour, eggs and salt until thick. Mix with cooked cold pastina and refrigerate overnight. Next day combine pineapple and oranges with Cool Whip and fruit cocktail (well drained).

Mary Petrelli
Giosue Carducci Lodge #226A

ITALIAN SHERBET

2 cups water
2 cups sugar
pinch salt

1 cup lemon juice
grated rind of 1 lemon
2 egg whites

Boil water, sugar and salt together 5 minutes over medium heat. Strain lemon juice into sugar syrup and add grated lemon rind. Cool. Beat egg whites until stiff but not dry and fold them gently into cooled syrup. Pour into freezing tray of refrigerator, cover with waxed paper and freeze until firm, about 3 hours.
Serves 6.

Joseph Sigillo
Rockland Lodge #2176

"S" COOKIES

4 large eggs
4 cups flour
4 heaping tablespoons baking
  powder

1 cup sugar
1 cup Wesson oil

Beat eggs, oil and sugar together. Mix in flour a little at a time. Roll out to 12-inch rope. Cut into 3-inch strips and shape into "S". Bake in 350° oven for 15 to 20 minutes.
Yields about 4 dozen.

Lorraine Craparo
LeAmiche Lodge #2550

TORTONI

1 cup almond or coconut
    cookies
¼ cup sugar
¾ cup milk

1 cup heavy cream
¼ teaspoon vanilla
¼ teaspoon almond flavoring

Roll cookies between wax paper to crush (reserve 2 tablespoons for topping). Combine crushed cookies, sugar and milk. Let stand for 10 minutes. Fold heavy cream, vanilla and almond flavoring into cookie mix. Put into cupcake liners (8 size cupcake baking pan) and freeze. Sprinkle tops with reserved cookie topping. After completely frozen, you can put them in plastic bags. Thaw slightly before eating.
Makes 8.

Evelyn Nelson
Loggia Glen Cove #1016

ANGINETTA

12 eggs
1 pound butter, softened
12 teaspoons baking powder

2 teaspoons lemon flavoring
2 cups sugar
3½ pounds flour

Icing:
1 stick melted butter
¼ cup water

1 pound confectioners sugar
1 teaspoon vanilla

Combine sugar, eggs and butter. Beat until smooth. Add lemon flavoring. Combine flour and baking powder. Add slowly, stirring until smooth. Dough should be soft. Add more flour if necessary. Turn on a floured board and knead. Shape into balls the size of a golf ball or make strips 4 inches long and wind a strip around three fingers to equal the size of a golf ball. Grease an oblong cookie sheet. Bake at 350° for 10 to 13 minutes or until lightly brown. Cool on racks, then ice and sprinkle with colored sprinkles.
This recipe is ideal for a party since the yield is about 200.

Grace Stanco
Loggia Glen Cove #1016

VANILLA COOKIES

5 cups flour
6 teaspoons baking powder
½ teaspoon salt
1 cup sugar

1 cup shortening (½ Crisco,
  ½ margarine)
2 beaten eggs in 1 cup of milk
2 teaspoons vanilla

To dry ingredients add shortening and mix like pie crust, then add eggs, milk and vanilla. Roll into small balls and bake at 375° for 10 to 12 minutes.

Frost when cool.

Rose Carozzoni
Italian American Women's Lodge #1979

CARMELLA'S PINK ITALIAN COOKIES

8 cups flour
1 cup sugar
3 tablespoons baking powder
¼ teaspoon salt
1½ teaspoons almond, anise or
  rum flavor

4 to 6 ounces red cherries,
  chopped
1 cup walnuts, chopped
1½ cups shortening
5 eggs
1½ teaspoons vanilla

Mix flour, sugar, baking powder and salt. Cut in shortening, cherries and walnuts. Make a well and add eggs, beaten with vanilla and flavoring of choice. Make a soft dough. Color with red food coloring.

Roll out and cut with small round (1- or 2-inch) cookie cutter or top of a whiskey glass.

Bake for 10 to 15 minutes in 350° oven. Cool and frost with glaze-type frosting, either vanilla or flavoring of choice used in cookie.

Judy Taverne
Utica Lodge #2054

ANISETTE CHIP BARS

½ pound butter, softened
 (or less)
1 cup sugar
4 eggs, beaten 1 at a time
1 tablespoon vanilla

1 tablespoon Anisette
4 cups flour
4 teaspoons baking powder
1 cup chocolate chips
1 cup chopped walnuts

Blend together softened butter and sugar. Mix in all remaining ingredients and form into a loaf. Place in a buttered pan and flatten out to ½-inch thickness. Bake at 350° 20 to 25 minutes.

Slice into bars and serve.

Victoria Gallello
Italain Heritage Lodge #2227

BLUEBERRY RICOTTA SQUARES

1 cup all-purpose flour
¾ cup sugar
1¼ teaspoons baking powder
¼ teaspoon salt
⅓ cup milk
¼ cup shortening
1 egg
½ teaspoon vanilla

1½ cups fresh or frozen
 blueberries, partially
 thawed
2 eggs
1¼ cups ricotta cheese
⅓ cup sugar
¼ teaspoon vanilla

In a small mixing bowl, combine flour, ¾ cup sugar, baking powder and salt. Add milk, shortening, 1 egg and ½ teaspoon vanilla. Beat with an electric mixer on low speed until blended. Beat on medium speed for 1 minute. Pour batter into a greased 9 x 9 x 2-inch baking; spread evenly. Sprinkle blueberries over batter.

In a medium mixing bowl lightly beat 2 eggs with a fork. Add ricotta cheese, ⅓ cup sugar, and ¼ teaspoon vanilla; beat until blended. Spoon ricotta mixture over blueberries and spread evenly. Bake in a 350° oven for 55 to 60 minutes or until a knife inserted near the center comes out clean. Cool. Cut into 16 squares. Store bars, covered, in the refrigerator.
Makes 16 servings.

Chris Parillo
Gabriele D'Annunzio Lodge #321

TARALLES (DE CONTE)

¼ cup olive oil
4 cups flour

6 eggs, separated
⅛ teaspoon baking powder

Beat eggs separately, yolks should be firm. Place flour on a board and make a well. Add yolks and whites a little at a time. Blend well and knead about 10 or 15 minutes. Cut a piece of dough and roll into a pencil shape, ¼-inch in diameter and about 6 inches long. Form a circle and pinch the ends. Shape all the dough and place on a covered surface.

Bring a large pot of water to a boil, drop a few taralles in the water (do not crowd them). Remove immediately as they start to surface. Place on white cloth and let dry 1 to 2 hours. Preheat oven to 500°. Put taralles on cookie sheet and bake 20 minutes until they have a golden color and have risen.

Icing:
1 cup confectioners sugar
1 teaspoon lemon juice

water as needed

Mix sugar, lemon juice and water as needed. Frost while taralles are warm.

Connie Conte
Enrico Caruso Lodge #2663

ITALIAN SOUR CREAM BISCUITS

2 cups margarine
2 cups sugar
4 eggs
6 cups flour
½ teaspoon baking powder

2 teaspoons baking soda
1 pint sour cream
1 teaspoon vanilla or anisette
chopped nuts, optional

Cream margarine, add sugar and eggs. Mix flour with baking soda and baking powder. Add flavor. Bake in 350° oven for 25 minutes. Remove from oven. Slice and brown for 10 or 15 minutes.
Makes 3 loaves.

Cecile Marra
Le Amiche Lodge #2550

CALZONGIE - CASSANDRA'S RECIPE

Filling:

1 can chick peas (boil to soften and mash in blender)
1 ounce or 1 square Baker's chocolate
½ cup sugar
¼ cup honey

1 teaspoon cinnamon
1 orange (grate rind - do not go into white pulp)
1 teaspoon of instant brown or black coffee
nuts (optional)

Pastry:

2 cups flour
¼ cup oil
1 teaspoon vanilla

⅛ cup sugar
dash of salt
lukewarm water

Mix all ingredients, knead and roll out to ⅛-inch thickness. Cut 3½-inch circles. Fill with one teaspoon of filling. Brush egg white around edges. Fold in half and press edges with fork.

Deep fry.
Yield: 24 filled cookies

Pauline Nocella
Italo Balbo Lodge #2361

ONGENETTE COOKIES

8 cups flour
14 teaspoons baking powder
1 cup oil

1 cup sugar
10 large eggs (12 if small)

In a large bowl, mix flour, baking powder and sugar. Make a well in center of flour mixture and add oil and eggs. Knead dough very well. Pinch off 1-inch pieces; place on cookie sheet. You can make a thumb print on top of cookie. Bake in preheated 350° oven for 10 minutes. Dip cookies in icing and sprinkle with colored confettini.

Icing:

1 teaspoon anise extract
1 cup confectioners sugar

hot water to desired consistency

Blend anise extract with enough hot water to the confectioners sugar to form smooth icing.

Barbara Lupo
Andrea Doria Lodge #2201

VENETIANS

1 (8 ounce) can almond paste
3 sticks butter, softened
1 cup granulated sugar
4 eggs, separated
1 teaspoon almond extract
4 or 5 ounces semi-sweet
　chocolate

2 cups sifted flour
¼ teaspoon salt
10 drops green food coloring
8 drops red food coloring
1 (12 ounce) jar apricot
　preserves

Grease 3 (13 x 9 x 2-inch) pans. Line with waxed paper; grease again. Break up almond paste in a large bowl with a fork. Add butter, sugar, egg yolks and almond extract. Beat with electric mixer until light and fluffy, 5 minutes. Beat in flour and salt.

Beat egg whites with electric mixer in small bowl until soft peaks form. With wooden spoon fold into almond mixture. Remove 1½ cups of batter; spread evenly into prepared pan. Remove another 1½ cups batter and add the green food coloring. Spread evenly into second prepared pan. Add red food coloring to remaining 1½ cups batter and spread into last pan. Bake in 350° oven for 15 minutes or just until edges are golden brown. Cakes will be ¼-inch thick.

Remove cakes from pans immediately onto large wire racks. Cool thoroughly. Place green layer on cookie sheet. Heat apricot preserves; strain. Spread ½ of the warm preserves over green layer to edges; slide yellow layer on top. Spread with remaining apricot preserves; slide pink layer on top, right side up. Cover with plastic food wrap; weight down with large cutting board. Place in refrigerator overnight.

Melt chocolate in a small cup over hot water or in microwave oven. Spread to edges of cake; let dry 30 minutes. If it stands longer chocolate will be hard to cut. Trip edges off cakes. Cut into small squares or rectangles.

Marcy Dabbene
William C. LaMorte Lodge #2251

184

RICOTTA COOKIES

2 sticks butter
2 cups sugar
1 pound ricotta cheese
2 eggs, slightly beaten
2 teaspoons vanilla

1 teaspoon baking soda
4-5 cups flour (first 2 cups with
    mixer, second 2 cups by
    hand)

Blend together butter and sugar. Add ricotta, blend. Add eggs slightly beaten, vanilla, 1 teaspoon baking soda and flour (first 2 cups with mixer, second 2 cups by hand). Work the dough, it should be on the soft side. If the ricotta is water, it will need more flour.

To the cookie mixture, you can add nuts, chocolate chips or coconut.

You can either roll or drop by teaspoon on greased cookie sheet. Bake at 350° for approximately 15 to 20 minutes. Top of cookie will spring to touch.

Frosting: (optional)
confectioners sugar
milk
lemon, orange, or almond

extract, or liquor, optional
nuts or coconut

Combine confectioners sugar and milk to consistency of your choice. Suggestions: You can add lemon, orange or almond extract, or liquor, to frosting. Top with nuts or coconut.

Gina Giovannelli
Daughters of Columbus Lodge #1666

SESAME SEED COOKIES

3½ cups flour
1 tablespoon baking powder
1 cup sugar
4 eggs

1½ teaspoons vanilla
3 ounces sesame seeds or more
½ cup margarine

Beat margarine, sugar and 3 eggs until light and fluffy. Add dry ingredients. Make a 6-inch rope, fold in half and twist. In a small bowl, mix remaining egg with 1 tablespoon water. Brush cookies with egg and dip in sesame seeds on wax paper. Place on ungreased cookie sheet and bake at 375°.

Rose Diorio
Daughters of Columbus Lodge #1666

PEPPER COOKIES

4 cups flour
1½ teaspoons salt
½ teaspoon pepper (add more
    for hotter cookies)

2 teaspoons fennel seeds
⅓ cup oil
1¼ cups warm water
1 package dry yeast

Mix warm water and yeast together and let stand.

Mix dry ingredients. Add water and yeast. Stir some by hand, add oil. Mix well and knead. Make into donut shape (thin). Brush with egg. Bake at 425° for about 25 minutes.

Carol Piccirillo
Gabriele D'Annunzio Lodge #321

ITALIAN NUT COOKIES

1 cup walnuts, chopped
¾ cup sugar
2 eggs

¾ cup oil (Wesson vegetable)
2½ cups flour
2 teaspoons baking powder

Bake walnuts on cookie sheet until slightly browned. Combine sugar, eggs, oil and nuts. Combine baking powder and flour. Mix flour mixture with other ingredients until all comes together. Place on cookie sheet in 2 long flat loaves. Bake at 350° for ½ hour. Take out of oven and allow to cool for about 1 minute. Cut diagonally into slices approximately ¾-inch slices and brown on each side for a few minutes at 350°.

Bea Donofrio
St. Francis of Assisi Lodge #2629

AMARETTI DI SAN VITO

1 cup (packed) almond paste
¾ cup sugar
3 egg whites

1 teaspoon grated lemon peel
1 tablespoon almond extract

Place everything in one bowl and mix at high speed for 5 minutes. Preheat oven at 325° for 30 minutes. Line cookie sheet with parchment paper.

¼ cup sugar

¼ cup pignoli nuts or sliced almonds

On a piece of wax paper, place sugar and nuts. Take teaspoonful of almond paste mixture and drop on wax paper mixture. With 2 fingers, pick up dough from wax paper and place on parchment paper, at least 1 inch apart. Place on bottom rack of oven. In about 10 minutes move pan to upper rack. Takes about ½ hour to cook.
Yield: 3 dozen.

Rose Tassone
Antonio Meucci Lodge #213

QUARESIMALE

1 pound special flour (buy at
    Italian bakery)
1¼ pounds sugar
1 teaspoon cinnamon
1 tablespoon vanilla

5 eggs
1¼ pounds almonds
2 teaspoons ammonia powder
    (buy at Italian bakery or
    substitute baking powder)

Mix everything in a bowl by hand. Divide dough in half. Take each half and divide again. You will have 4 quarters and it will be sticky. Use 12 x 15-inch cookie sheets. Place parchment paper on cookie sheet. Make loaves with dough and place 2 on each sheet. Bake in 325° oven for 40 minutes. After 15 minutes, alternate cookie sheets in oven. Put top one on bottom rack and bottom one on top rack of oven. Beat 1 egg and brush loaves with egg. Place in oven for additional 15 minutes. Remove. Cool for 10 minutes only. Cut into 1-inch slices.

Rose Tassone
Antonio Meucci Lodge #213

GARLIC CHIP COOKIES

10 cloves garlic
½ cup maple syrup
1 cup butter, softened
¾ cup brown sugar
¾ cup sugar
2 eggs

1 teaspoon vanilla
½ teaspoon salt
2½ cups flour
1 teaspoon baking powder
2¼ cups chocolate chips
½ cup chopped nuts

Drop garlic cloves into boiling water for about 5 minutes until tender. Peel and chop garlic and soak in maple syrup for 20 minutes. Cream butter, sugars, eggs and vanilla together until light and fluffy. Combine flour, baking soda and salt. Add to creamed mixture. Then stir in chocolate chips and nuts. Drain garlic and add to cookie batter. Blend well. Drop batter by tablespoons onto ungreased cookie sheet 2 inches apart. Bake at 375° for 8 to 10 minutes, until lightly browned. Cool on racks.
Makes 5 dozen cookies.

Nicky Maccarulo
Rockland Lodge #2176

WALNUT CRESCENTS

1 cup butter or margarine,
    softened
⅓ cup sugar
1 teaspoon vanilla

2 cups flour
½ cup chopped walnuts
sifted powdered sugar

Cream first 3 ingredients and 1 tablespoon water. Stir in flour and nuts; mix well. Shape into crescents. Place on ungreased cookie sheet. Bake at 350° for 15 to 20 minutes. Cool on rack. Roll in powdered sugar.
Makes 60.

Rosemarie Putrino
Daughters of Columbus Lodge #1666

RUTTURA'S MILLION DOLLAR COOKIES

1 cup margarine
½ cup white sugar
½ cup brown sugar
1 egg
2 cups flour

1 teaspoon cream of tartar
1 teaspoon baking soda
½ teaspoon almond extract
½ teaspoon vanilla

Cream together shortening and sugars, mix in egg.

Sift together dry ingredients and work into first mixture. Add flavorings.

Drop by teaspoon on cookie sheet and press thin with glass bottom which has been greased and dipped in sugar. Bake in 350° oven for 8 to 10 minutes.

Alice Ruttura
Enrico Fermi Lodge #2150

OLGA'S ITALIAN COOKIES

6 eggs
1 cup sugar
4 cups flour
4 teaspoons baking powder
½ teaspoon salt

¾ cup oil
orange rind from 1 orange,
    grated
2 teaspoons lemon juice
1 teaspoon vanilla

Beat together egg and sugar until blended. Mix together flour, baking powder and salt. Add flour mixture to egg mixture alternating with oil until all mixed. Stir in orange rind, lemon juice and vanilla. Drop by level teaspoonfuls onto ungreased cookie sheets. Bake at 350° for 8 to 10 minutes or until light tan color. Do not brown. Cool on racks. When cool, ice with following:

powdered sugar
water

vanilla (to taste)

Mix all together to consistency of thick glaze, thick enough not to run off cookies.
Yield: 4 to 5 dozen.

Olga Cannizzaro
Aida Ladies Lodge #2163A

189

MARIE TESORA'S ITALIAN COOKIES

8 eggs
1½ cups shortening (3 sticks),
   melted
1 cup sugar

1 ounce lemon extract
2 pounds flour
8 tablespoons baking powder

Beat together eggs, shortening, sugar and lemon extract. Add flour and baking powder to egg mixture in a large bowl. After mixing, knead on a lightly floured board. (Mixture appears moist but works itself out.)

Roll and shape into cookies. Bake in a 350° oven for 10 to 12 minutes (Do not overcook.)

Glaze by dipping into confectioners sugar icing.

Icing:
1 pound confectioners sugar
½ ounce lemon, anise or
   vanilla extract

warm water for desired
   consistency

Mix confectioners sugar, extract and a little warm water.

Maria Tesora is a deceased member of the Heritage Lodge #2227

Mae Scarangella
Aquileia Ladies Lodge #935

PIGNOLI COOKIES

1 pound almond paste
2 cups granulated sugar

4 egg whites, slightly beaten
8 ounces pignoli nuts

Cut the almond paste into small pieces and place in small bowl or mixer. Beat it for a minute or two until it is smooth and soft. Slowly add the sugar and beat well. Add egg whites and continue beating until smooth. Place 2 cookie sheets 1 on top of the other (this will prevent excessive browning) and cover with a sheet of parchment paper. Place mixture in a pastry bag and using a ½-inch tip, pipe mixture onto the paper or drop by tablespoon onto baking sheet leaving 1 inch between them.

Sprinkle each cookie with several pine nuts and bake in 350° oven for 20 minutes or until lightly browned.

When cookies are done, remove from parchment paper immediately using a sharp knife dipped in hot water. If the cookies stick to the parchment paper, wring out a towel in hot water and lay it out flat on the counter. Place the parchment paper on the wet towel and wait a few minutes. The moisture will loosen the cookies enough to remove them.

Makes about 60 cookies (2 pounds)

Pauline Nocella
Italo Balbo Lodge #2361

SOFT ANISE COOKIES

6 eggs
½ cup shortening
½ cup butter or margarine
2 cups sugar
1 cup milk

6 cups flour
6 teaspoons baking powder
pinch of salt
2 tablespoons anise extract

Mix flour, baking powder and salt together. Cream shortenings and sugar together. Add eggs, then anise extract. Alternate milk and flour mixture until well blended. Drop by teaspoons on greased cookie sheet. Bake in 350° oven for 8 to 10 minutes. Frost as desired.

Mary Teresa Purtell
Giosue Carducci Lodge #226A

ANISE BISCOTTI

3½ cups flour
1 cup sugar
2 teaspoons baking powder
4 eggs

1 teaspoon anise seeds
2 tablespoons whipped butter,
   at room temperature

Mix first 3 ingredients in large bowl. Add eggs and mix well. Add anise seeds, and whipped butter. Mix well and shape into four rolls, slightly flattened. Put on greased cookie sheet. Bake approximately 30 to 40 minutes or until light golden in color at 350°.

Remove from oven and cut into slices. Put back on cookie sheet, cut side down. Bake approximately 20 minutes or until light golden. Turn cookies over to other side and bake again.
Makes approximately 70 cookies.

Mary DiScala
Cellini Lodge #2206

NANCY'S BISCOTTI

6 large eggs, separated
1 cup sugar
1 cup oil
3 teaspoons baking powder

3 teaspoons vanilla
1 teaspoon salt
3 cups flour
1 cup walnuts

Beat each egg 3 minutes, one at a time. Add sugar; beat until blended. Add oil and vanilla, stir until blended. Mix flour, baking powder and salt; sift together, then add to other ingredients. Fold in walnuts. Mix well. Shape into 3 loaves and put onto a greased baking sheet. Bake in 350° oven for 10 to 12 minutes. Cut into slices; flip each over on its side and bake for another 5 minutes or until lightly browned.
Makes 60 biscotti.

Nancy Codella
Aquileia Ladies Lodge #935

RICETTE PER LE SANTE FESTE

FESTE

HOLIDAY RECIPES

NEW YORK OSIA FILIAL LODGES

•**Guy Lombardo Lodge #2417**, Ronkonkoma, Charter issued 1978: Guy Lombardo was the leader of one of the most popular dance orchestra's of all time, The Royal Canadians. His rendition of "Auld Lang Syne" at midnight on New Year's Eve has become a national institution for many years.

•**Daughters and Sons of Italian Heritage Lodge #2428**, Brooklyn, Charter issued 1978: This lodge is dedicated to the preservation of our beautiful Italian Heritage.

•**Giglio Di San Antonio Lodge #2432**, The Bronx, Charter issued 1979: The Giglio is a flowered pedestal, sometimes several stories high, and atop is Saint Anthony.

•**Father Donald B. Licata Lodge #2435**, Carmel, Charter issued 1979: This lodge was named after the National Chaplain and New York State Chaplain of the Order Sons of Italy in America, Donald B. Licata, a priest of the Archdiocese of New York. For over a decade, Father Licata has been the adopted spiritual father of OSIA.

•**John A. Prudenti Lodge #2442**, East Patchogue, Charter issued 1979: John A. Prudenti, a deceased community activist, exemplified the goals of the Order and demonstrated loyalty and devotion to family, country and friends. He contributed to many charitable and civic associations in the community.

•**Michelangelo Lodge #2451**, Hampton Bays, Charter issued 1980: Michelangelo Buonarroti was one of the greatest figures in the history of art. He was a sculptor, painter, poet, architect and military engineer. He designed the dome of St. Peter's, sculpted the "Pieta" and the statue of "David". His greatest work remains the frescoes on the ceiling and high altar of the Sistine Chapel in the Vatican in Rome.

•**Brian Piccolo Lodge #2467**, Bayville, Charter issued 1980: Brian Piccolo was one of the great football running backs of the Chicago Bears and played in the backfield with the great Gayle Sayres. He was Sayre's roommate and close friend. At age 26, Brian Piccolo was stricken with cancer and while dying in a hospital in Chicago, Gayle Sayres was receiving the MVP award. It was at this awards ceremony that Sayers made an impassioned speech to the audience and asked them to pray for Brian Piccolo. Brian's story is memorialized in the movie "Brian's Song".

•**Mario Lanza Lodge #2491**, Middle Village, Charter issued 1981: Alfred Cocozza (Mario Lanza) had an unusual tenor voice which won him national acclaim as a radio concert and recording artist. His great talent was exhibited in both classic and operatic music.

•**Jimmy Durante Lodge #2514**, Brooklyn, Charter issued 1981: This lodge was named after Jimmy Durante, the beloved Italian-American comedian and entertainer.

•**Father Francis Bressani Lodge #2548**, Amsterdam, Charter issued 1983: Father Francis Bressani was the first Italian in the Mohawk Valley. He was a scholar, popular preacher and a heroic Jesuit who labored to Christianize the Indians in the 1640's and 1650's. He was captured and tortured by the Iroquois and is memorialized with a plaque at the Auriesville Martyrs' Shrine.

•**Le Amiche Lodge #2550**, Yonkers, Charter issued 1983: The name Le Amiche was chosen for its feminine form "the friends" in Italian. Their motto is "Speak up, Be Heard, Be Friends".

•**Donatello Lodge #2559**, Westbury, Charter issued 1984: Donatello was a Florentine sculptor of the early Renaissance. He is best known for his statues of David and St. John the Baptist.

(Continued on final page of recipes)

NEW YEAR'S DAY SOUP ITALIAN STYLE

5 cups chicken broth
1 large chicken breast
1 small bunch parsley
½ cup Italian bread crumbs
½ teaspoon oregano
1 teaspoon salt
¼ teaspoon ground pepper
2 tablespoons Parmesan
  cheese, grated

¾ pound beef, ground sirloin
  or chuck
1 egg
1 large carrot
1 small bag fresh spinach
1 can condensed cream of
  celery soup
1 small box bite-sized ravioli,
  cheese-filled

Put chicken broth into a 4-quart soup pot with cover and bring to a slow boil. Slice chicken into strips ½-inch wide. Add to stock. Chop parsley and add half to stock.

In a large bowl, mix ingredients for meatballs as follows: Bread crumbs, oregano, salt, pepper, grated cheese, remaining parsley and water. Mix and let stand for 1 minute. Mix in ground meat and egg, roll into small bite-sized balls. Using electric fry pan (350°) or medium heat on the stove, fry in oil until light brown on all sides. Drain on paper towels, add to stock. Cover and simmer 1 hour. Peel and cut carrots into slices, cut spinach into about 1-inch pieces. Add to stock and cook ¾ hour. Add soup and cook 15 minutes, covered. Cook ravioli, drain well and add to stock just before serving.

Note: Other vegetables can be used, such as string beans, mushrooms and turnips.

Marie Stets
Stella D'Argento Lodge #1916

PASTA CON SARDE

1 pound fresh sardines
1 bunch broccoli, chopped
1 (29 ounce) can Hunt's tomato
  sauce
1 medium onion, diced
1 can anchovies
2 tablespoons olive oil

1 (15 ounce) Condimento
  Completo per Pasta Con
  Sarde (complete seasoning
  for macaroni with sardine
  can be purchased in Italian
  delicacy store)
1 pound imported ziti pasta
pepper
toasted bread crumbs

Parboil broccoli and chop into medium pieces. Set aside.

In 6-quart saucepan, sauté onion in olive oil until golden. Add anchovies, stirring until paste like. Add tomato sauce and ½ can of water. Bring to boil. Add Condimento Completo per Pasta con Sarde and broccoli. Bring back to boil.

Add fresh sardines. Pepper to taste. Bring to boil, lower to simmer until sardines break into small pieces.

Cook ziti according to directions. Blend sauce and pasta thoroughly. Allow to set 5 to 10 minutes. Sprinkle with toasted bread crumbs.

Toasted Bread Crumbs:
1 cup bread crumbs
3 to 4 anchovies fillet
¼ cup Locatelli cheese

2 tablespoons olive oil
pepper

Heat oil. Add anchovies, blend until paste like. Add bread crumbs, pepper to taste, and cheese. Stir constantly over medium heat until crumbs are thoroughly toasted.
Yield: 4 servings.

Pasta con Sarde is a traditional Sicilian dish served on St. Joseph's Day, March 19th.

For 3 generations, Pasta con Sarde has been the main course at the St. Joseph's Day celebration in the Cangemi family. No meat is served at this meal.

Michelina Cangemi
Donatello Lodge #2559

SAINT JOSEPH CREAM PUFFS I

½ cup shortening
⅛ teaspoon salt
1 cup boiling water

1 cup sifted flour
3 eggs

Filling:
1 (15 ounce) container ricotta
    cheese
¼ cup confectioners sugar

1 teaspoon vanilla
¼ teaspoon lemon rind

Add shortening and salt to boiling water and stir over medium heat until mixture boils. Lower heat and add flour all at once and stir until mixture leaves sides of the pan.

Remove from heat and add 1 egg at a time beating thoroughly after each addition. Shape on an ungreased cookie sheet using 1 teaspoon or 1 tablespoon of paste for a puff.

Bake in preheated oven at 450° for 20 minutes, then reduce temperature to 350° and bake about 20 minutes longer.

Remove from oven and place on rack to cool. When puffs are cold, cut tops off and fill with ricotta cream made as follows:

Ricotta Cream: Add confectioners sugar, lemon rind and vanilla to ricotta cheese and blend. Replace puff tops and serve, sprinkled with confectioners sugar and topped with ½ maraschino cherry.

Marion Moretti
Giosue Carducci Lodge #226A

SAINT JOSEPH'S DAY CREAM PUFFS II

Puff Pastry:

1 cup hot water	1 cup sifted flour
½ cup butter	4 eggs
1 tablespoon sugar	1 teaspoon grated orange and
½ teaspoon salt	lemon peels

Pineapple Cream Filling:

1½ cups milk, scalded	½ cup cold milk
½ cup sugar	3 eggs
2 tablespoons cornstarch	1½ cups crushed pineapple
⅛ teaspoon salt	1 teaspoon vanilla

For Pastry Puff: Beat together first 5 pastry ingredients. Beat vigorously with a wooden spoon until mixture leaves sides of pan and forms a smooth ball (about 3 minutes). Remove from heat. Quickly beat in, one at a time, beating until smooth after each addition, 4 eggs.

Continue beating until mixture is smooth and glossy. Add, mixing thoroughly, grated orange and lemon peels.

Drop by tablespoonsful 2 inches apart on the baking sheet. Bake at 450° for 15 minutes. Lower heat to 350° and bake 15 to 20 minutes longer or until golden brown. Remove to rack to cool. Cut a slit in side of each puff and fill with your favorite filling. One of our favorites was Pineapple Cream filling.

Filling: Scald in top of double boiler 1½ cups milk. Meanwhile, sift together into saucepan, sugar, cornstarch and salt. Add ½ cup cold milk stirring well. Gradually stir in scalded milk. Stirring gently and constantly, bring cornstarch mixture rapidly to boiling over direct heat and cook for 3 minutes. Pour into double boiler top and place simmering water. Cover and cook about 12 minutes, stirring 3 or 4 times. Stir about 3 tablespoons hot mixture into 3 eggs which are slightly beaten. Immediately blend into mixture in double boiler. Cover over simmering water 3 to 5 minutes. Stir slowly to keep mixture cooking evenly. Remove from heat. Cover and cool.

Then stir in crushed pineapple and vanilla. Chill in refrigerator.

Grandma always made these puffs for us on March 19th, the Feast of St. Joseph. However, she only used a coal stove or the brick oven in the back yard.

Gloria Ruggiero-Trofinoff
St. Francis of Assisi Lodge #2629

EASTER RICE PIE

2½ pounds ricotta cheese
1 cup rice, cooked
1 teaspoon anisette extract
1 teaspoon vanilla

1 cup sugar
6 eggs
½ pint heavy cream

Mix all together, for best results mix ricotta and sugar first. Put in a greased pie pan and bake for 1 hour until done at 350°.

Rose DiLorenzo
Ann Bambino Lodge #2353

EASTER WHEAT PIE

1 can asti cooked wheat
¼ cup hot scalded milk
¼ teaspoon salt
¼ teaspoon sugar
1¼ pounds ricotta cheese
1 cup sugar

6 egg yolks, beaten
1 tablespoon orange water
¼ cup diced citron
¼ cup diced orange peel
4 egg whites, beaten stiff
1 teaspoon vanilla

In scalded milk, mix can of wheat, salt and sugar (¼ teaspoon of each). Boil for 5 minutes and remove from heat. Add citron, orange peel and set aside.

Meanwhile, beat ricotta and sugar. Add 6 egg yolks, vanilla and orange water. Blend well. Stir in prepared wheat. Fold in beaten egg whites and pour into pie shell. Arrange pie crust strips criss-cross over filling to edge. Roll bottom overhang up over strips at edge and flute heavily.

Bake in preheated oven at 350° for 1 hour or until firm in center. Let cool in oven with door open. Serve sprinkled with powdered sugar.

Happy Easter!

Norma DiTrapani Pettus
Per Sempre Ladies Lodge #2344A

GRANA PIE

4 eggs
1 teaspoon vanilla
¾ cup sugar
1½ cups ricotta cheese
1 cup cooked wheat (¼ cup
   raw) (must use skinless
   wheat)

peel of 1 whole orange, grated
¼ cup citron, cut or grated
1 cooked or pre-packaged
   9-inch pie shell

Soak wheat 1 to 2 hours. Cook wheat for 1 hour or until wheat shell cracks open. Drain and let cool completely.

In a large bowl, mix sugar, eggs and vanilla. Add ricotta cheese and mix well. Add cooked wheat, orange peel and citron. Mix well. Pour mixture into prepared pie shell.

Bake in 350° oven for 1 hour or until knife comes out dry.

Anne and Rose Marano
Marco Polo Lodge #2214

EASTER BREAD

1 dozen eggs
2 sticks melted margarine
1½ cups sugar

1 tablespoon each vanilla and
   lemon
¾ teaspoon salt
about 8 cups flour

All ingredients used must be at room temperature. Dissolve 1 package dry yeast in ¼ cup warm water. Add to the above ingredients and beat until mixture pulls away from spoon. Cover with wax paper and cloth and let rise at least 6 hours (or overnight). Punch down and let rise second time until doubled in size. Divide dough in half and place in a greased pan. Wait until dough rises to the top and bake at 325° for 1 hour. Use two (10-inch) tube pans.

Carmela Persico
Gabriele D'Annunzio Lodge #321

GRANDMA MARCHIANO'S EASTER MEAT PIE

1 loaf of fresh pizza dough or
   bread dough

Filling:

2 pounds ricotta cheese
6 eggs
1 (8 ounce) package mozzarella
   cheese, shredded
½ pound ham
½ pound peccoli salami
½ pound pepperoni
¼ pound prosciutto
pepper and grated Parmesan
   cheese to taste

Roll out dough using flour and line 2 (9-inch) pie plates.

Cut up all meats into small chunks and set aside.

In mixing bowl, add ricotta and gradually add eggs, shredded mozzarella and meats. Mix well and add pepper and Parmesan cheese to taste. Place mixture into pie plates and cover top with a thin layer of dough. Bake at 325° for approximately 1 hour or when golden. Important: Puncture top layer of dough for air.

Let set until cool. Delicious with a glass of red wine.

This recipe was written up in the Long Island Newsday *on March 27, 1994 in the Food Day Section.*

Dominick G. Giordano
Cellini Lodge #2206

MARY'S PIZZA RICOTTA

12 eggs	1 pint heavy cream
12 heaping tablespoons sugar	3 tablespoons citron
3 pounds ricotta cheese	6 tablespoons rum or anisette

Preheat oven to 320°. Divide above ingredients into 3 parts to allow portions to fit into your blender container. Turn blender on low and then high until ingredients are mixed and liquid.

Pour into a 12½ x 10⅝ x 2¾-inch pan (not necessary to grease pan). Place in preheated oven for 45 minutes to 1 hour.

Try not to open oven door more than twice. When a knife is put into the center and comes out clean, place a clothes pin in the door opening to allow the cake to cool. It can be removed from the oven in 1 hour.

Usually made at Easter time.

Easy and delicious!

Dolores Altomare
Romanesque Lodge #2198

GRANDMA MISURACA'S PASTA DI SAN GIUSEPPE

1 (16 ounce) can chick peas	¼ cup extra virgin olive oil
1 (16 ounce) can cannellini beans	1 pound egg noodles or homemade pasta
1 head of cauliflower, chopped	1½ cups split peas (optional)
2 heads of broccoli, chopped	salt and pepper to taste
1 head fennel (finocchio), chopped	

Bring broccoli and cauliflower to a boil. If using dried beans instead of canned, boil them separately. When broccoli and cauliflower are nearly done, add finocchio, oil, salt and pepper.

Boil pasta separately. When pasta is done add pasta and beans to the vegetables.

Serve with grated Parmesan or Romano cheese.

Marc J. Randazza

ORANGE ANISE BREAD

1 package dry yeast	1 teaspoon orange rind
¼ cup water	3 eggs, beaten
4 to 5 cups flour	1 teaspoon orange extract
¼ cup sugar	1 teaspoon vanilla extract
2 tablespoons shortening	¾ cup warm milk
2 teaspoons anise seed	1 egg, beaten, for glaze

In small bowl, dissolve yeast in warm water. Combine 4 cups flour, sugar, anise seed, orange rind and shortening in large bowl. In a separate bowl, combine 3 eggs, orange extract, vanilla extract and warm milk. Make well in center of flour, pour softened yeast and egg mixture into well. Mix thoroughly, adding as much of the remaining flour as needed to make soft dough. Place on floured surface and knead until smooth and elastic; this will take about 10 minutes. Put in a lightly greased bowl, turn greased side up and cover. Let rise until double, 2 to 3 hours.

Punch down and divide dough into 6 equal parts for 2 small braids or into 3 equal parts to make 1 large braid. Shape each section into 12-inch long rope, tapered at ends. For each braid, line 3 ropes 1 inch apart on lightly greased cookie sheet. Braid loosely without stretching dough, beginning in middle and working toward either end. Seal ends well. Cover and let rise about 30 minutes, or until double. Brush with beaten egg and bake in a preheated 375° oven for 30 to 40 minutes.

This recipe is not solely reserved for Easter. It is absolutely delicious with baked ham.

Chris Parillo
Gabriele D'Annunzio Lodge #321

RICOTTA AND RICE PIE WITH PINEAPPLE

Dough:

2 cups flour	2 eggs
3 teaspoons baking powder	⅓ cup milk
¼ cup granulated sugar	1 teaspoon vanilla
½ cup vegetable shortening	½ teaspoon orange extract

Filling:

1 cup raw rice	1 (8¼ ounce) can crushed
2 cups milk	pineapple, drained well
1 pound ricotta cheese	grated rind of 1 orange
4 eggs	grated rind of 1 lemon
¾ cup granulated sugar	juice of 1 lemon
3 tablespoons flour	1 teaspoon orange extract
	2 teaspoons vanilla

To make dough: Combine dry ingredients. Cut in shortening until flour resembles coarse meal. In a separate bowl, combine eggs, milk, vanilla and orange extract. Add to dry ingredients and mix to form soft ball. Chill covered for 1 hour.

Meanwhile, preheat oven to 350° and prepare filling. Cook rice according to directions on package. Add milk to hot rice and set aside to cool. Break up ricotta cheese with pastry blender. Add eggs one at a time, beating well after each addition. Add sugar and beat well. Fold in rice, flour, drained pineapple, grated orange and lemon rind and flavorings.

Divide the dough into 2 portions, use ⅔ for the 10-inch pie and the remaining ⅓ for the 8-inch pie. Refrigerate smaller portion of dough until ready to use. Break ⅓ off the larger dough and set aside. Roll dough between 2 sheets of waxed paper that is lightly sprinkled with flour, adding more flour if necessary. Fit pastry to line 10-inch pie dish. Roll out reserved dough and cut into ½-inch wide strips. Put ⅔ of filling in pie shell and cover with strips to make lattice topping. Crimp edges. Repeat procedure with remaining dough and filling to make 8-inch pie. Bake for 45 to 50 minutes, until top is lightly brown and pie is set.

This sweet version of an Italian Easter Pie is enough for 2 pies; an 8-inch and a 10-inch pie.

Chris Parillo
Gabriele D'Annunzio Lodge #321

CHESTNUTS

With a sharp knife, make cross slits on the flat side of each chestnut. Place into a shallow pan. Bake at 400° for 15 minutes, tossing chestnuts occasionally.

Serve hot.

Chestnuts are traditionally served during Thanksgiving.

Virginia Johnson
America Lodge #2245

CUCCIA

1 pound dried chick peas
1 pound of wheat kernels

3 quarts of water
salt to taste

Place chick peas and kernels in separate pots with water. Soak overnight.

Drain water and replace with fresh cold water, add salt and bring to boil. Stir, lower heat. Cover and simmer slowly for 1 hour or until tender but firm. Mix chick peas and wheat to your preference. Serve hot with olive oil and black pepper or cold with sugar, cinnamon and milk.

St. Lucy's Day Favorite - December 13th.

Nancy Romano
Giovanni Caboto Lodge #2372

BAKED NUTS

2 egg whites, beaten until
**   frothy**
1 stick margarine

1 pound shelled walnuts
1 cup sugar
dash salt

Melt margarine in a 9 x 13-inch pan. Add salt and sugar to egg whites. Fold in walnuts and blend together. Bake at 325° for 20 minutes. Break into pieces as soon as it's taken from the oven.

This was a favorite Christmas Eve snack just before going to midnight Mass.

Gloria Ruggiero-Trofinoff
St. Francis of Assisi Lodge #2629

CHRISTMAS EVE TOMATO SAUCE

oil (enough to fully cover bottom of large saucepan)
3 gloves garlic
1 pound filberts (hazelnuts)
1 pound walnuts
1 can pitted black olives
1 medium size jar pitted green olives
1 small jar capers (preferably in water; if you use dry, salted ones, rinse some of the salt off before using)
¼ cup pine nuts
2 cans flat anchovies
3 large cans crushed tomatoes

Place oil and garlic cloves in pan. Simmer until garlic browns.

Cooking over low heat, add the filberts, turning continuously. When they turn a golden brown, add walnuts. Stir constantly. When the walnuts begin to turn a golden brown, add remaining ingredients, stirring constantly. Remove garlic. Add the tomatoes.

Mix well. Bring to a quick boil. As soon as the sauce begins to bubble, cover the pot and lower the heat to a simmer. Cook for 2 hours.

Remember to stir the sauce every 5 to 10 minutes to prevent sticking and burning.
This will yield enough sauce for 2 pounds of spaghetti. Traditionally only linguine or spaghetti are served with this sauce.

This sauce is the traditional sauce prepared and served by the Nolani (people from Nola, Italy) on Christmas Eve.

Sylvia Summa
Daughters and Sons of Italian Heritage Lodge #2428

EGG NOG BREAD

1 cup quick-cooking oats
1¾ cups flour
1 teaspoon baking soda
¼ teaspoon each baking
   powder, cinnamon and
   nutmeg

½ cup butter, softened
¾ cup sugar
2 eggs
1 cup eggnog
½ cup white raisins

Mix first 6 ingredients together and set aside. In mixer beat butter and sugar until creamy, add eggs and beat well. Add oat mixture and eggnog alternately to creamed mixture beating well after each addition. Mix in raisins. Pour batter into a greased and floured loaf pan. Bake in 350° oven for 45 minutes or until toothpick comes out dry. Cool completely on wire rack before removing pan.

Traditionally served on Christmas Eve.

Jeanette Bonardi
Romanesque Lodge #2198

FRUIT CAKE

2 cups chopped walnuts
1 (3½ ounce) jar candied
   cherries (cut in quarters)
2 cups light or dark raisins
3½ cups sifted all-purpose
   flour
1½ teaspoons baking powder
½ teaspoon salt

1½ cups butter or margarine
   (¾ pound)
2 cups sugar
7 eggs
1 teaspoon vanilla
½ cup bourbon or whiskey
   (I use whiskey)

Preheat oven to 350° oven. Use 10-inch tube pan greased and floured well. Combine walnuts, cherries, raisins and bourbon or whiskey and let stand overnight. Sift flour with baking powder and salt. Beat butter, sugar and vanilla until light and fluffy. Add eggs one at a time beating well. Mix in flour mixture until smooth. Add fruit and mix with wooden spoon to combine well. Turn into prepared pan; smooth top with spatula. Bake in center of oven for 1 hour and 10 minutes. Cool on wire rack for 20 minutes. Turn on wire rack and cool completely.

When completely cool, wrap in foil and refrigerate for several days.

Dorothy Unold through Joseph E. Fay
Santa Rosalia Lodge #2131

CHRISTMAS FRUIT CAKE

1 pound dates, cut up
2 cups pecans
2 cups walnuts
1¼ cups flour
1 cup sugar
½ teaspoon salt

2 teaspoons baking powder
5 eggs, slightly beaten
1 teaspoon vanilla
1 (10 ounce) jar candied
    cherries, include green

Mix fruit and nuts. Mix dry ingredients, eggs and vanilla. Pour batter over fruits and nuts and mix until well coated. Pour into well greased angel food pan. Bake 1 hour at 325°.

Bridget Zaino
Donatello Lodge #2559

CRUSTELE

(Bow Ties)

3 cups flour
12 eggs
12 tablespoons sugar (6 regular
    and 6 powdered)

12 teaspoons oil
1 grated lemon rind
1 tablespoon baking soda

Start with 3 cups flour to make a soft dough consistency. Mix in other ingredients. Roll out, cut into strips. Intertwine each cut strip and deep fry in oil until golden. Powdered sugar may be added by sprinkling on after removing from oil.

"For any special occasion or Holiday."

Grace Ferrara
Cellini Lodge #2206

HOLIDAY CHERRY CHEESE BARS

Crust:

1 cup walnut pieces, divided
1¼ cups all-purpose flour
½ cup firmly packed brown
    sugar

½ cup butter-flavored Crisco
½ cup flaked coconut

Filling:

2 (8 ounce) packages cream
    cheese, softened
⅔ cup granulated sugar
2 eggs

2 teaspoons vanilla
1 (21 ounce) can cherry pie
    filling

Heat oven to 350°. Grease 13 x 9 x 2-inch pan with butter-flavored Crisco. Set aside.

Chop ½ cup nuts coarsely for topping. Set aside. Chop remaining ½ cup finely.

For crust: Combine flour and brown sugar, and cut in butter-flavored Crisco until fine crumbs form. Add ½ cup finely chopped nuts and coconut. Mix well. Remove ½ cup and set aside. Press remaining crumbs in bottom of pan. Bake at 350° for 12 to 15 minutes, until edges are lightly browned.

For filling: Beat cream cheese, granulated sugar, eggs and vanilla in small bowl at medium speed of electric mixer until smooth. Spread over hot baked crust. Return to oven. Bake for 15 minutes longer. Spread cherry pie filling over cheese layer. Combine reserved coarsely chopped nuts and reserved crumbs. Sprinkle evenly over cherries. Return to oven. Bake 15 minutes longer. Cool. Refrigerate several hours. Cut into bars about 2 x 1½-inches.

Gloria Colantone
Ann Bambino Lodge #2353

STRUFOLI I

2 pounds flour	**2 teaspoons vanilla**
10 eggs	**2 teaspoons baking powder**
1 stick butter or margarine, melted	**1 large jar honey**

In a large bowl beat eggs, add vanilla and butter. Put flour into another bowl and add egg mixture. Knead dough and let set in covered bowl for 10 minutes. Repeat twice. When dough is ready, cut into small pieces. Roll dough into strips and cut into ½-inch pieces. Deep fry and add honey and candy sprinkles.

Nettie Innella
John Michael Marino Lodge #1389

STRUFOLI II

2 whole eggs	**1 teaspoon vanilla**
2 egg whites	**2 cups flour**
4 tablespoons sugar	**½ teaspoon salt**
4 tablespoons corn oil	**1 teaspoon baking powder**
1 tablespoon white vinegar	**1 medium size jar honey**
3 tablespoons rye whiskey	

Beat together whole eggs, egg whites and sugar. Add oil, vinegar, whiskey and vanilla and continue to beat. Add flour, salt, baking powder and mix to soft dough. If dough is too sticky to handle, add more flour to make it workable. Knead dough for a few minutes on a lightly floured board.

Take small pieces of dough and roll into pencil shape. Cut into pieces (size of chick peas) and fry in hot oil until golden brown.

Pour honey into a large pot and bring to a boil, when honey is thinned out, add strufoli balls and stir. Remove from heat and pour from pan onto platter. Form a mound and decorate with colored sprinkles.

Josephine Paduano
Jane H. Landi Lodge #2239A

CUCCIDATI

(Fruit Filled Cookies)

Crust:

2 cups flour
1 teaspoon baking powder
¼ cup sugar
8 tablespoons shortening

2 eggs, slightly beaten
2 tablespoons water
   (approximately)

Filling:

½ pound raisins, put through
   coarse chopper
½ pound dried figs, put
   through coarse chopper
½ pound citron, cut into small
   thin slices

½ cup almonds, toasted and cut
   small
¼ cup walnuts, coarsely cut
few pine nuts, if desired
1 teaspoon cinnamon
¼ cup honey

Mix ingredients of crust as for biscuit dough. Roll out ⅛-inch thick and cut into rectangles 2½ to 4 inches and 8 x 4 inches. Put filling in center of each and moisten edges well with water, fold together over top and seal edges. Place folded side down on greased baking sheet and pull dough into horseshoe shapes and letter S and with a knife, notch the outer parts of the S shape to the filling and slit the dough over the filling in a few places where the filling will show through. The square pieces can be shaped into birds, fish and flowers notching the dough to represent feathers and fins and petals. Brush tops with an additional egg (beaten) and bake in hot oven at 425° for about 18 to 20 minutes. Sprinkle with powdered sugar when slightly cool.

Rita Petrillo La Piana
Donne d'Italia Lodge #2330

AUNT CLARA'S ALMOND CHRISTMAS COOKIES

1 pound powdered sugar	2 pounds flour
5 or 6 eggs	1 pound butter
2 pounds softshelled almonds	grated rind and juice of 1
or 1 pound shelled almonds	lemon

Mix ground nuts and sugar together until fine. Set ¾ cup aside for top of cookies. Add flour and butter and mix well. Add eggs saving 1 yolk for the top of the cookies. Add grated rind and juice of one lemon. Let dough stand in cool place overnight. Roll dough very thin and cut out forms. Put on ungreased cookie sheet. Smear top with egg yolk mixed with milk. Sprinkle with mixture of nuts and sugar. Bake at 375° for 8 to 10 minutes or until golden brown.

Frances D'Angelo
Loggia Glen Cove #1016

ITALIAN CHRISTMAS COOKIES

Dough:

2 cups sugar	1 pound ricotta cheese
½ pound butter	4 cups flour
1 teaspoon salt	3 teaspoons vanilla
1 teaspoon baking soda	3 eggs

Butter Cream Frosting:

1 pound powdered sugar	⅛ teaspoon salt
¼ pound butter	1 teaspoon vanilla
2-4 teaspoons milk	

Dough: Cream butter and sugar; add eggs. Beat, add vanilla, ½ teaspoon flour, salt, baking soda and ricotta cheese then the rest of the flour.

Drop teaspoonsful of dough on ungreased cookie sheet. Bake at 350° for 15 minutes; frost when cool.

Frosting: Cream butter, salt and sugar. Add vanilla and milk. Blend together. Decorate with food color.

Fran Cuda
Italian American Women's Lodge #1979

HOLIDAY NOUGATS

2⅓ cups whole unblanched
   hazelnuts
2 cups whole unblanched
   almonds

1 cup honey
2 egg whites
1 cup sugar
2 tablespoons water

Oil two 8 x 8-inch cake pans. Toast hazelnuts and set aside. Place honey in top of double boiler and cook for 1 hour. Remove honey from heat. Beat egg whites stiff until peaks are formed. Add beaten egg whites to honey, 1 tablespoon at a time, beating well with a wooden spoon after each addition.

Combine in a light colored skillet, 1 cup sugar and 2 tablespoons water. Bring to boiling over medium heat and cook, stirring occasionally, until caramelized. Add caramelized sugar to honey mixture, a tablespoon at a time, mixing well after each addition. Remove mixture to heavy saucepan. Stirring constantly, cook over direct heat to 240° (soft ball stage) or until a small amount forms a soft ball in cold water. Remove from heat while testing. Add, all at once, hazelnuts and 2 cups whole unblanched almonds. Mix well and quickly pour into greased pans. Cool 20 minutes. Cut nougats into pieces and wrap in wax paper.

This was a special favorite of Grandma's. She would wrap these candies in colored paper and hang on a special "candy Christmas tree" for the "Little Christmas" or the "Epiphany." The candies were supposed to be for the "Three Kings" as they brought their gifts to the Baby Jesus. However, the kings always left enough candy for us kids!

Gloria Ruggiero-Trofinoff
St. Francis of Assisi Lodge #2629

NEW YORK OSIA FILIAL LODGES

•**Edward J. Speno Lodge #2568**, East Meadow, Charter issued 1984: Edward J. Speno was a Senator from Nassau County who served as Chairman of the New York Transportation Committee and advocated a safety car. The design, by Republic Aviation Corporation, was named "the Spenomobile".

•**St. Thomas Aquinas Lodge #2569**, Hauppauge, Charter issued 1984: St. Thomas is the Patron of scholars and theologians. He remains the most influential theologian/philosopher in all Christendom and is known for his two great works, the "Summa Contra Gentiles" and the "Summa Theologica". He was a Dominican friar and preacher.

•**Giuseppe Garibaldi Lodge #2583**, Eastchester, Charter issued 1986: Giuseppe Garibaldi was an Italian Freedom Fighter who led an army of men called "Redshirts" to liberate Sicily and Southern Italy to achieve the unification of Italy in 1861. Garibaldi was offered a Union Command by President Abraham Lincoln, but refused since Italy was still not unified.

•**John D. Calandra Lodge #2600**, Yonkers, Charter issued 1987: John Calandra was a New York Legislator who served in the State Senate. He chaired the committee to investigate discrimination at City University of New York and the Italian American Center at CUNY was later renamed the Calandra Institute after he passed away.

•**Anthony Casamento Lodge #2612**, West Islip, Charter issued 1988: Corporal Anthony Casamento waited 38 years to receive his Medal of Honor for conspicuous gallantry and intrepidity at the risk of his life, above and beyond the call of duty, while serving with company "D" First Battalion, Fifth Marines, First Marine Division on Guadalcanal. The Order Sons of Italy in America was instrumental in assisting Brother Casamento in obtaining his medal from President Jimmy Carter.

•**St. Francis of Assisi Lodge #2629**, Beacon, Charter issued 1989: St. Francis of Assisi "Il Poverelle" can easily be called the International Ecumenical Saint. People of many races and creeds revere him because of his love of animals and all God's creations. St. Francis of Assisi is the patron saint of the Order Sons of Italy in America.

•**Raffaello Lodge #2661**, Middletown, Charter issued 1992: This lodge is named after one of Italy's most famous painters and architect. He was one of the greatest artists of the Italian Renaissance and is buried in the Pantheon in Rome.

•**Enrico Caruso Lodge #2663**, North Fork, Charter issued 1992: This lodge is the most Eastern lodge in the State of New York. It was named in honor of Enrico Caruso, one of the greatest operatic tenors of all times. His voice was described by many as "gold swathed in velvet" and through the years, Caruso developed a repertoire of more than forty operas.

•**Philip Torchio - Con Edison Lodge #2664**, Long Island City, Charter issued 1992: Named after a Vice President of Consolidated Edison who was born and educated in Como, Italy. He held many engineering patents and was active in community affairs including serving as the Mayor of Bronxville.

•**Michael Valente Lodge #2667**, Long Beach, Charter issued 1993: World War I Medal of Honor recipient, Valente was a life long resident of Long Beach.

•**Figlia D'America Lodge #2674**, Cobleskill, Charter issued 1993: The "Children of America" lodge was the first lodge formed in the Cobleskill area in over a decade.

•**Father John Papallo - Kings Park Lodge #2684**, Charter issued 1994: A Capuchin Franciscan and talented singer, Father Papallo served in the Kings Park parish and worked in hospital ministry on Long Island. He was killed in a car accident in 1989 at the age of 46.

INDEX

215

H

HOLIDAYS

L

LAMB

P

PASTA

V

Order Sons of Italy in America
New York Grand Lodge Foundation, Inc.
Bellmore, New York 11710-5605

YES — I am proud of my Italian heritage and I want to be a member of OSIA.

The Order Sons of Italy in America (OSIA), founded on June 22, 1905 in New York, is the oldest, largest, and most demographically diverse organization representing men and women of Italian heritage in North America.

OSIA and two subsidiary organizations, The Commission for Social Justice, Sons of Italy Foundation, work to preserve the rich cultural heritage of Americans of Italian descent; cooperate with U.S. and Italian organizations to strengthen trade, business, and educational opportunities between North America and the European community; represent the interests of Italian-American families, young professionals, students, and retirees before the U.S. Congress; and strive to promote the positive contributions of Italian-American men and women.

OSIA's one-half million family members nationwide represent a broad cross section of the Italian-American community. Many are involved in OSIA activities at the national level, in one of OSIA's 850 local chapters, or as at-large members through their home state. Men and women share equal status within OSIA, as do individuals of all professions and ages.

Benefits of your OSIA At-Large Membership

OSIA provides Italian-Americans and their families with unique opportunities and benefits, including:

- A personal subscription to the monthly *OSIA News*, the national newspaper.
- Scholarship opportunities at the local, state, and national levels.
- Opportunities to join OSIA's influential voice in domestic and international affairs.
- Participation in local, state, and national social, business, and political networks.
- Discount travel programs.
- National mentoring and Washington internship programs.
- Involvement in Italian-American culture through lectures, films, book discussion groups, Italian language courses, and folk life programs.
- Opportunities to participate in a variety of special events and social programs.
- Insurance coverage for you and your family at low group rates.
- An outlet for volunteer energies and professional expertise.

Additionally, as an at-large member in the state of New York, you will receive:

- A personal subscription to the bi-monthly *Golden Lion*, the New York State newspaper.
- An official OSIA membership lapel pin.
- An official certificate of membership.
- The privilege of attending local chapter meetings with visitor status.

I'm interested in joining the oldest and largest organization representing Italian-Americans, the OSIA. I have enclosed payment for one-year's membership.

Name _____

Address (home) _____

City _____ State _____ Zip _____

Telephone _____

Occupation _____

Company or School _____

Work or School Address _____

City _____ State _____ Zip _____

Telephone _____

Membership levels $50 ☐ regular member $20 ☐ Student member

I wish to pay by _____ check (payable to *Grand Lodge of New York*)

CUCINA CLASSICA

O.S.I.A. New York Grand Lodge Foundation, Inc.
2101 Bellmore Ave.
Bellmore, New York 11710

Please send _____ copies of *Cucina Classica* @ $16.95 each _____
Postage and handling @ $3.75 each _____

Name _____

Address _____

City _____ State _____ Zip _____

Make checks payable to OSIA N.Y. Grand Lodge Foundation, Inc.

- -

CUCINA CLASSICA

O.S.I.A. New York Grand Lodge Foundation, Inc.
2101 Bellmore Ave.
Bellmore, New York 11710

Please send _____ copies of *Cucina Classica* @ $16.95 each _____
Postage and handling @ $3.75 each _____

Name _____

Address _____

City _____ State _____ Zip _____

Make checks payable to OSIA N.Y. Grand Lodge Foundation, Inc.

- -

CUCINA CLASSICA

O.S.I.A. New York Grand Lodge Foundation, Inc.
2101 Bellmore Ave.
Bellmore, New York 11710

Please send _____ copies of *Cucina Classica* @ $16.95 each _____
Postage and handling @ $3.75 each _____

Name _____

Address _____

City _____ State _____ Zip _____

Make checks payable to OSIA N.Y. Grand Lodge Foundation, Inc.